A
Pacific Northwest
Publisher

ISBN-10: 0982858787

ISBN-13: 978-0-9828587-8-3

Published by Broken Publications.
www.BrokenPublications.com

Cover Image by Eleanor Leonne Bennett
http://EleanorLeonneBennett.zenfolio.com/

Cover layout: Jennifer-Crystal Johnson
www.JenniferCrystalJohnson.com

Edited by Jennifer-Crystal Johnson

For more about Soul Vomit and the annual anthology, go to www.SoulVomit.com or follow on Facebook at www.facebook.com/soulvomitanthology.

Soul Vomit

Beating Domestic Violence

Table of Contents

Foreword
By Jennifer-Crystal Johnson

First and foremost, I want to say a big thank you to those of you who are reading this book, have purchased it in show of support, or are simply showing an interest in the often silent epidemic of domestic violence that happens behind closed doors all over the world every single day. It's not easy to read about... it's actually pretty uncomfortable in some cases. But if it were a comfortable topic, then it wouldn't be a problem, would it?

My mission in publishing this annual anthology is to bring to light some of the typical experiences of men and women suffering through abuse on a daily basis. Soul Vomit was created to give a voice to victims who are still stuck, survivors who have gotten out and want to help make a difference by telling their story, and to serve as a warning to young men and women everywhere that love isn't always sunshine and rainbows, nor is it always meant to last... nor is it always enough.

Thinking back, I always felt that if my parents or I had known about some of the signs of an abuser, things would've turned out much differently for me personally. I also know that everything happens for a reason, though, and I wouldn't give up my kids for five lifetimes of sunshine and rainbows. I do feel it's important to shed light on the topic, especially to give people in general an idea of what kinds of emotional torment someone who has been abused will go through during – and after – an abusive relationship. It is my hope that understanding and family support will increase, psychological disorders can be addressed more quickly, and children can be better cared for with such a support system in place.

Most abuse survivors have long-term emotional issues such as anxiety, depression, post-traumatic stress disorder, sexual disorders originating from spousal rape or molestation, and a number of other psychological and emotional afflictions that may or may not get better over time. This varies for everyone. Without a general understanding of these long-term effects, people who have never experienced domestic violence will not understand a victim's reactions, behavior, or emotional standpoint about specific things.

Unfortunately, there isn't very much help out there for survivors once they're out of their abusive situation, nor does the abuser have to answer to their actions unless charges are pressed for physical violence. Survivors of domestic violence are therefore often emotionally and mentally crippled, have a hard time getting or keeping a job, and often live in poverty for the rest of their lives because no one acknowledges that post-traumatic stress disorder inflicted by an abuser has no benefits attached, no disability claim, and no way of even being proven. This essentially means that the abuser gets away without repercussion (which also means the abuser can maintain a certain control over the victim), and for many abusers, this means they win. That's the only thing that matters: power and control through the use of fear and "winning." Though not everyone will agree, I feel that an abuser is incredibly insecure, which translates into pushing others down – especially those who begin with a sense of confidence – and making them completely dependent. This allows the abuser to get whatever they want, usually without a fight, and it serves them as a superficial way to feel secure and needed even though they aren't *really*.

With this being said, there are only a handful of ways to create the change necessary to offer abuse survivors help in achieving some semblance of a normal life: awareness, understanding, and empathy through outreach and privately-funded programs. Some state-run programs have been made available in the US; however, during an economic recession or depression, many of the programs aimed at help and outreach lose funding, sometimes up to 80%, as was the case with certain programs in my area.

Again, the best way to help is to raise awareness and help people who have never been in a domestic violence situation see what a DV victim goes through so that ordinary people shed their apathy and have a connection – even if it is only through literature, art, stories, and poetry. Though imagining abuse is nowhere near the real thing, I firmly believe that the imagination is extremely powerful and can allow us to see beyond our personal experiences.

A single phone call to the police could be the difference between life and death for a domestic violence victim and his or her children. If this book can inspire such a connection and be the nudge for that single phone call that could save a life, then it has served its purpose.

As I read through the submissions for this project that is so personal to me, I went through a range of emotions. Some of the work gave me terrible chills because I know all too well what these emotions that are described herein feel like. Some made me smile with a guilt-inducing sense of vengeance... oh, the thoughts that wander through a victim's mind when their abuser isn't looking. Others made me feel that much more compelled to publish this book and shove it in the world's face so people know what goes on, even long after you leave an abuser. And all too often, I was in tears while working on putting this book together, especially when reading some of the submission letters themselves.

It amazes me how so many different stories and experiences can have such similar emotional undertones. Or maybe I should say riptides... because these emotional undertones aren't easily forgotten for those who have been there. As a matter of fact, they attach to your heart and brain as if someone had stuck them to your forehead with a pushpin. The main emotions are always the same: fear, guilt, shame, anger, worthlessness.

There are very specific stories that I can relate to on a deeply personal level, while others are slightly more removed from my experiences. I found it interesting to read about other abusers being obsessive about hair, for example. Why is a woman's hair so important that she is told she is forbidden to cut it or change it? Why must it always stay the same?

When reading some of these stories and poems, I hope you'll remember that domestic violence, spousal rape, abuse, and the use of fear and control as a means to dictate lives are not pretty, romantic, or pleasant. Let this also serve as a disclaimer: there is adult language, graphic description, and violence within these pages. That is the nature of this particular beast. But even if it makes you uncomfortable... even if it makes you cringe, gives you chills, makes you cry, induces nausea, or pisses you off, I encourage you to read it and remember that people go through this each and every day, all over the world.

This collection is for those people. Hope is still there, inside your heart. No one deserves to be abused and I hope that the strength portrayed in these pages seeps out into you, whether you've left already or are still trapped.

Things to Keep in Mind

Each piece within these pages has a purpose and was chosen for a reason. There are many different voices here with many different perspectives; some more blunt than others, some more artistic, and some will throw you for a loop. Hopefully all of them will inspire thought or shed light on the issue at hand.

If you or anyone you know is in a domestic violence situation and you're seeking help, please call the National Domestic Violence Hotline at 1−800−799−SAFE (7233) or TTY 1−800−787−3224.

You may also seek help online at www.thehotline.org.

Trail Etiquette
By Bernard Hafeli

It was summer rain, in most respects the same as the spring, fall, and winter rain, just warmer. It felt good to be out in it. Since it wasn't cold, the hood of his jacket dangled down his back, letting the rain trickle through his hair and down his face, occasionally blurring his vision so the spindly purple and orange flowers that waved in the breeze resembled emaciated arms beckoning him off the road and into the Douglas firs. Once in a while, a BMW or Volvo sluiced past over the slick blacktop, sending a rooster tail of mist up to greet the down-falling drops. The people driving the cars were the same people he saw on the bus into the city, the same ones who filled the elevators in the downtown high-rise that harbored Livingood Advertising, his current place of employ.

They were people with enough money to own a nice semi-pricey house amid the tree-choked acreage of Mercer Island, plopped down like a mound of misplaced rainforest in the middle of Lake Washington. Only today, instead of the worsted suits and waterproof raincoats they usually donned to make their mark in the corporate world, they favored faded jeans and flannel shirts and shiny rain slickers, and their quest wasn't for untapped niche markets and accelerated growth stratagems, but salmon and wine and chanterelle mushrooms. Because today was Saturday, and as Harry watched the people out in the rain, walking their dogs, pruning their rosebushes, he was fairly certain their lives were better than his. They seemed content and reasonably happy, and if not happy at least accepting of their individual lots, and if not accepting at least they probably weren't stuck in relationships where ceramic bookends got bounced off their heads. He rubbed the crease above his right eye. There was still a dull pain beneath the puffy, puckered ridges, a not-so-subtle reminder of the previous night's rollicks.

The truth was he never knew what might happen. He could come home after work and find Sharon lounging come-hitheringly on the sofa, wineglass in hand, wine seductively a-swirl, having put the finishing touches on an epicurean tour de force replete with de rigueur fruits, cheese, and bottles of Napa's latest small-pressing finds. Music would waft up the wooded hillside to greet him at the carport after a long day of ad making. There would be tentative laughter and halting conversation that grew richer and fuller as it became understood by both parties that an armistice was in effect, that this night was to be a return to more tractable times, before the failings in each of them found focus in the faults of the other. Later there would be hours of abandoned lovemaking.

Other nights were different. He'd arrive home and find Sharon staring out at the slate gray lake, jaw clenched, steely daggers of light in the pupils of both eyes. Those were nights to beware. Something had happened during the day to pick away at the scab of the everyday and expose the deep cut beneath, the rift between the way things were and the way they ought to be, the way—they were both becoming increasingly aware—they'd never be. On nights like this, she'd usually ingested more than a few drinks by the time he got home. He'd quickly catch up. The rest of the night was like walking on S-shaped peanuts of Styrofoam, trying not to make them squeak. If they were both lucky, it would be an evening of wary glances and unfinished sentences. If not, merry hell could be in session. Sometimes the police were summoned by neighbors. But luckily, the house was remote enough that the sounds of strained voices, slammed doors, shattered china, and battered stereos were usually only a nuisance to the birds and raccoons.

Last night, he'd come home with Copper River salmon, a loaf of sourdough, and four bottles of wine—an expensive Chardonnay, a touted Merlot, and two jugs of cheap screw-top.

"Sharon?" he'd called from the kitchen, where he plopped down the groceries, the flute of sourdough sticking up like a fat finger of warning.

No answer.

He opened one of the jugs and guzzled down the dry, flat wine.

"Sharon?"

When he entered the living room, he could hear the hair dryer droning like a hive of tired bees. He went to the bathroom door and knocked.

"Sharon, I'm home."

"I'll be out in a minute."

He went back to the kitchen. The whisker-hands on the cat-face clock pointed to six-fifteen. Motes of dust and cat dander drifted among the ochre evening light pouring through the rain-flecked windows. He took another dose of wine and wondered if it would be a night of reconciliation or retribution. He suspected the latter, since he hadn't come home until 3 a.m. the night before in an attempt to stave off a confrontation that had been brewing over an upcoming trip back to see Sharon's brother, a trip he was hoping to dodge. With the bottle still held aloft, Sharon walked up from behind.

"Hope you bought more."

"I did," he burbled, lowering the jug. "There's plenty."

"Where were you last night?"

"I worked late. I left a message."

"You worked until after midnight?"

"It was after three when I got done."

"I don't believe you."

"That doesn't change the fact I did."

"Liar."

Harry smiled. It was stupid. It just pissed her off but he couldn't help it.

"You are such a prince, Harry. The prince of pointless bullshit."

"Sharon, don't start."

"Asshole."

She noticed the salmon on the counter. She went over, picked it up, raised it over her head with both hands like a priest making an offering to the Heavenly Father, then flung it end over end through the air until it smacked down on the linoleum floor.

"Son of a bitch!" she screamed. "Get the hell out!"

And Harry got the hell out. He took the flagstone steps two at a time up to the carport, arriving out of breath and at a loss. How did he get in this insane relationship? He went to the plastic garbage can full of grass clippings, reached in, and pulled out the pint of Royal Gate vodka he kept hidden there. He opened the bottle and tilted it heavenward, chugging until his eyes watered and he started to gag.

He'd spent the night sleeping in the car parked in the carport, which was risky business because lately she'd been coming up to see if he left or not. He awoke once to her angry, contorted face inches from his own, screaming. Another time he opened his eyes to find her quietly watching him, a look of genuine puzzlement on her face, profoundly sad. That had been worse. But last night she'd left him alone, and he was grateful. When he woke up this morning, there was the warble of birds and spatter of rain on the carport roof. But when he went down to the house to assess the damages, and perhaps make amends—it was Saturday after all, the weekend needn't be a total ruin—he'd heard the water of the shower through the bathroom door and her voice murmuring, growing steadily fiercer, continuing the theme of the night before. So he'd decided to leave, to take a walk and let emotions cool. He planned to return by nightfall. By then, the righteous fires might well be doused. After a few days, the two of them might decide they were even still, at least a little bit, in love. That was the odd thing about this relationship—how wildly it swung from one extreme to the other. Bipolar—that's how he thought of it.

Another car slickered by. A Saab. He wondered what he looked like to the people inside. "Mommy, why is that man walking in the rain? He's getting all wet." He felt like a pariah. Hung over, bleary-eyed, dripping with rain, he did not uphold the island's chevron of sober respectability. Nowhere near. If this were two months ago, he would just have taken the car, but due to an unfortunate drunk driving arrest, that was no longer an option.

Up above, he heard a high-pitched scree, austere and otherworldly. When he looked up, an eagle was wheeling through the damp, leaden sky, its white head like another bird entirely, hitching a ride aboard the black, outstretched wings. Usually, they avoided areas this populated, but he'd seen them on this end of the island twice before. There was a secluded stream not far away that gushed into the lake. Someone told him the eagles were born near the stream, and that, like salmon, they were programmed to return to their place of origin.

The eagle carved a wide arc then veered down into the woods. Harry decided to follow. This part of the island was carpeted with acres of open forest, separating its big-windowed, custom-built homes. A series of trails honeycombed through the trees. Sometimes people rode horses along the trails, but today, with the chronic rain, the paths were left to the squirrels and the slugs, and the occasional wayfarer like Harry.

Once he quit the road there was no sign of the eagle. But the woods still held an allure. In the past, he'd set off on trails like this and wound up in wholly unexpected places, discovered things about the island he wouldn't have otherwise known. It was on a day like this that he met the old man with the Russian accent who showed him the hidden stream and told him about the eagles. Another time he'd happened upon a field marked by two rotting hay wagons and an old pickup truck. Near the truck was the foundation of a house that must have burned and a hardscrabble graveyard. One marker read: Karl, ?—1933, Always Worth His Oats. Harry was unsure whether Karl had been a farm worker or a horse. Two small headstones were inscribed "Fluffy" and "Pretty Girl," so the family did, apparently, honor their animals. Harry was hoping for a similar diversion today, something to wrest his attention and occupy his thoughts before the grim certitude of facing up to what could be done about his seriously damaged relationship.

Upon entering the woods and quitting the hard-packed dirt of the road shoulder for the spongy mulch of the forest path, his step grew lighter. He began to hypothesize a life with a higher ratio of joy. If his marriage came apart, he'd move to British Columbia and live in the coastal mountains. He could work on a local newspaper or drive a school bus. He wouldn't need much money. And he would definitely cut back on the drinking, which he couldn't deny was becoming more of a problem. The memory of crashing the Audi, despite the distance of two months, was still disconcertingly vivid. Being brought back to consciousness by the policeman rapping at the window, motioning for Harry to open the door. Seeing himself in the rearview mirror, blood pasted to his forehead, highlighting an angry purple bruise. The policeman helping him up the hill. At the top, another policeman, an emergency van, about twenty gawkers. It had been a warm, sunny day, unlike today, the first nice weather after months of dribbling rain.

"Are you okay?" the paramedic asked.

"I think so. My ribs hurt."

They wiped off his face, beamed a light in his eyes, pressed his ribs until he gasped with pain. He couldn't pass any of the sobriety tests. When he stuck out his hands like a tightrope walker and tried to walk the white line, he listed abruptly to the left.

"Look at the drunk man," the little girl said. She was with her father, whose eyebrows rose and forehead furrowed—what could he say? Because the girl was right. Harry was the drunk man.

He spent the night in jail and appeared in court the following morning. He got sentenced to a treatment program in lieu of being locked up, lost his license, and acquired a probation officer named Bert. He was forbidden to partake of any alcohol for two years, which, of course, was impossible. He had a drink that afternoon.

But that was precisely what he was trying not to think about. Better to concentrate on the misty gray day, the dripping, fragrant forest, and the inviting trail that curved through the thicket of shiny,

19

sharp-leafed holly much like another path once had for Hansel and Gretel, or so he imagined.

Suddenly, he stopped. Directly in front of him, perched on a stump, sat a woman. Her eyes were closed and her head moved dreamily back and forth, to music, it seemed, only she could hear. She wore no socks or shoes. She looked familiar, like someone he'd seen on the bus into the city. Only then, her loose black hair would have been piled on top of her head, her lips glossed red, her body tucked into a business suit. She'd have been reading the financial section of the local paper. He thought he may have seen her in the state liquor stores, too—the one on the island or the one downtown or the large one over in Bellevue. Lately, he'd been spreading his purchases around. He wasn't sure how closely his probation was being monitored and he didn't want the store clerks to notice. He wondered if she was doing the same, alternating stores to allay suspicion.

She hadn't noticed him. He could still turn around and leave. But instead he moved closer, a decision that made him feel like a voyeur, getting off on the fact that he could see her in this private moment while she had no inkling he was there. He didn't like the feeling. He shook the holly bushes to get her attention.

"Hello," he said.

But he said it too softly, as if only part of him wanted to announce his existence. She didn't respond, but continued swaying, softly singing a song he couldn't place. He approached slowly, until he stood directly before her. Still she didn't respond. He reached out to touch her hesitated, then grabbed her by the arm.

"Hey, hello."

The singing stopped. Her whole body jerked. She blinked and looked around.

"Who are you?" she asked, shaking free of his hand.

"I was walking by and saw you."

Her eyes were opaque. Her face was scratched, as if she'd been walking through prickers and briar.

"What happened to your shoes?" he asked.

She looked at her bare feet. They were smeared with mud and pine needles. She shook her head and looked off down the trail.

"I don't know how I got here," she said.

"Do you live nearby?"

The question seemed to puzzle her. "I'm not sure," she said, looking around, as if for the first time. "Are we on Mercer Island?"

"We're on the southwest end, near the road that goes to the supermarket."

She took a deep breath then let it go. She looked at Harry.

"I must have wandered off," she said.

She was pretty, Harry decided, even drooped over a tree stump with her black hair hanging in lank, damp strands, her eyeliner streaked across her cheeks like bitter tears. He guessed she was in her mid-thirties, close to his own age.

"Maybe you should go home and change into something dry," he said. "I can help get you on your way."

She stared at him now, as if trying to divine his intentions. Were they purely Samaritan, or did he plan to waylay her off in the bushes? Or did she think him presumptuous, suggesting he could help get her on her way? Or was she simply of the mind that it was none of his damn business, that he should keep his nose where it belonged?

"Okay," she said finally.

She stood up abruptly then plunked back down on the stump.

"My legs fell asleep," she said. "Give me a minute."

She began swinging her legs, first one then the other, and massaging her knees.

"You must think I'm pretty weird," she said, "out all alone in the rain with no clear idea why."

"Well, it's a little out of the ordinary," he said. "But I'm out alone, too. I just remembered to wear shoes."

He held out his hand. "I can help you get going until the blood starts to flow."

She stared at his hand. "You seem nice enough. But isn't that a common trait of psycho-killers? They seem nice when you first meet them?"

She took his hand and stood up. As she did, he slid his other arm around her to steady her on the path. She stepped back and regarded him closely.

"You're not a psycho-killer. I've seen you on the bus."

"I work downtown. My name is Harry. But I don't think riding the bus disqualifies you as a psycho-killer."

"Maybe you're right. I should be more careful."

She started walking down the path. Harry followed close behind.

"You don't seem like a Harry," she said. "You seem like a Dave or maybe a Jeff."

"You seem like an Ann-Marie."

"That's two names," she said.

"You seem a bit complex."

For a while, no one said anything. There was the sound of the rain, the rustle of branches, the slap of her bare feet against the wet dirt.

"Are we going the right way?" Harry thought to ask.

"I don't know," she said. "These trails all look the same."

It turned out they weren't going the right way. They ended up down by the lake and had to double back and take another trail.

"Now we're getting somewhere," she said. "I remember these berry bushes with all the cobwebs."

The bushes were meshed with the silky lace. Dense drops of water separated from the branches above and periodically punched holes in the shimmery webbing.

"How do you know it was these bushes?" Harry asked. "There are lots of berries in these woods. Lots of spiders, too."

"Good point," she said. "I could be wrong. That's been known to happen."

They came upon a ten-foot cyclone fence that blocked their way.

"Woops," she said. "I've led us astray."

"This fence surrounds something," Harry said. "Probably somebody's house. If we stay with the fence, it should lead us to some access road or driveway, which should take us to a road."

They followed the fence through a field of yellow mustard, then a grove of fir trees that the rain had washed clean, their bark dark and steaming, their scent sharp and invigorating, enough to dissolve the reside of Harry's hangover and make him glad, for the moment, to be alive.

Finally, they encountered the main road that bisected the island.

"Okay," she said. "We're good. I know the way from here."

They paralleled the road but stayed back among the brush. Every so often a driveway would appear, cutting back to a house they sometimes caught a glimpse, sometimes they saw nothing at all.

"You could have left bread crumbs," he said.

"I did," she said. "Those seagulls must have been hungry." Her thin face had lost most of its pallor.

"You never told me your name," Harry said.

"Why did you say Ann-Marie before?"

"You reminded me of someone."

"Harry, you won't get very far with a woman if you tell her she reminds you of another woman."

"Good point," Harry said. "So tell me your real name and I can stop making mistakes."

"That would ruin everything. Then you couldn't have your way with a woman you didn't know the name of."

She was walking ahead of him and looked back over her shoulder.

"You are going to have your way with me, aren't you? Before you murder me?"

She was starting to make Harry uncomfortable. The joke was wearing thin.

"I'm sorry," she said. "I'm creeping you out. I've been told I have that effect."

She stopped walking and faced Harry.

"My name is Erin," she said. "And to tell you the truth, things are just a wee bit crazy, Harry."

After that, she felt the need to explain. She took psych meds, she said, for her clinical depression. Her doctor had her on a new one and the dosages weren't right. Last night, she was having after-dinner drinks with her husband and they'd had an argument of the name-calling, object-hurling variety. He'd stomped into the other room to make a phone call. That was the last thing she remembered.

"What time was that?"

"About eleven."

"That's twelve hours unaccounted for."

"It's happened before. Once, I came to in the middle of knocking on someone's door. When it opened, a woman I didn't know asked me what I wanted."

"What did you say?"

"I told her I wanted to borrow some vodka. She thought not."

He wasn't sure how much this to believe. When he'd had his arm around her earlier, she'd smelled like a distillery. He didn't know if you were supposed to drink when you took psych meds, but he did know you weren't supposed to drink a fifth of vodka.

By now they'd left the road and were back on a trail to which she'd led. To the right was a small ravine. On the other side, a large three-story house began to appear, with wooden decks abutting the top two levels. Floor-to-ceiling windows and sliding doors looked out on the surrounding greenery. It was all glass and metal and treated wood, Scandinavian in feel. It must have cost a fortune.

"We're here," Erin brightly announced.

"Wow," Harry said. "What do you do for a living?"

"We're drug dealers," she said. "Don't tell."

As they descended the ravine, he noticed things, toys mainly—a big-wheel tricycle tipped over in the mud, giant building blocks in primary colors, a soccer ball, a plastic baseball bat.

"Do you have kids?"

"They're Derek's from a previous marriage. Sometimes they come visit."

They walked across the thick, damp grass to a sliding door. Laid out before it was a two-tiered patio, formed of uneven slabs of dark gray slate, which must have felt cold to Erin's bare feet. She hurried across them. She swooshed the door open and stepped inside.

"Derek?"

She motioned for Harry to follow her in. He went as far as the door and stuck his head inside. It was as far as he intended to go. He just wanted to say goodbye. It felt awkward to just leave.

But she had disappeared down a hallway.

"Yoo-hoo," he heard her say, her voice fainter, part of the house. "Anybody home?"

Against his better judgment, he waited for her to return. If Derek was gone, Harry was at the point in the day where a quick drink or two would set rather nicely with his long walk home. The room he was gazing into was a sort of recreation room. A beige-and-brown-plaid sofa, matching chairs, and a wicker coffee table surrounded a big-screen television in one corner of the room. A ping-pong table dominated the middle ground. On the walls were framed posters advertising European wares from earlier in the century—bicycles, aperitifs, hats, luggage.

He stepped into the room to inspect a poster of a French-looking waiter holding aloft a tray on which sat an imp. The imp was red and leering and his hands held up two glasses filled with red liquid. "Vov" read the message curved across the top of the poster. Harry was leaning in close to read the fine print—to see if he could make out whether "Vov" was a liqueur or an elixir or just what, exactly—when he heard an angry shout.

"Where the fuck have you been?"

There was a slap and a cry of pain. Harry froze. He should have left. He turned and eyed the sliding door.

24

"Damn you, Erin!"

Another slap was followed by a loud thud. The wall shook. Harry moved quickly in the direction of the noise, down the hall toward a doorway bathed in light. When he entered, a man turned and looked his way.

"Who the fuck are you?" the man shouted.

Erin sat slumped on the floor, one hand one her chin, moving it tentatively back and forth. The man was thin, with long sandy hair beginning to go white. Angry blotches of pink colored his otherwise ashen face. Behind him was a wide table. On the table sat a metal butcher's scale and a collection of clear plastic baggies filled with white powder. There were a lot of baggies.

"Erin, who is this asshole?"

"He isn't anyone, Derek. Calm down." She pushed herself to her knees, then rose slowly to her feet. "He found me in the woods. He helped me get home."

Derek walked to the far end of the room, so the table stood between himself and Harry. He opened a drawer and reached inside. He pulled out a gun. He pointed the gun at Harry.

"How the fuck can I leave him alone, Erin, when he's seen what he's seen here? Here, where you brought him to see it. You are such a fucking airhead."

"Oh Christ, you sound like a movie gangster, Derek. Put the gun away. Your very hard and steely, very manly gun."

She moved unsteadily around the table until she was behind Derek, and then disappeared out the doorway at the back of the room. Seconds later, a water faucet started running.

Derek barely noticed. He stared at Harry. Wariness slowly took the place of anger in Derek's eyes. He raised the gun level with Harry's face. Harry tried not to jump. He'd never looked into a gun barrel before. It wasn't like the cop shows. He couldn't think of any witty words to toss in Derek's direction—no James Bond, he. The truth was he was more frightened than he'd ever been. Everything slowed to a crawl. He wondered if Derek had ever shot anyone. He prayed he wouldn't piss in his pants.

"Well, what do we do now?" Derek said.

"Let's forget this ever happened," Harry heard himself say. His voice seemed to come from a long way away—California, maybe, where he wished more than anything he was right now. It sounded disconnected, his voice, a sound byte from a movie promo. Had he really said that? Let's forget this ever happened?

Derek smiled. "Now you sound like a bad actor," he said. "What's your name?"

Harry couldn't decide whether to lie or tell the truth. A lie could throw Derek off the scent if he ever came looking for Harry—that is if Harry could somehow escape this present predicament, which, at the moment, seemed dubious. Weighing against the lie was Harry's ability to tell it convincingly—he was nervous, after all—plus the fact that Derek could simply check Harry's wallet, discover Harry was lying, and become even angrier than he'd previously been.

"Christopher," Harry said, not technically a lie since it was his middle name.

"Let's see your wallet."

By now, Erin was reentering the room. As Harry reached for his wallet, she approached Derek from behind, slowly, one careful step at a time, whatever sound she made drowned by the water still spilling from the faucet. In her right hand was a bowling trophy that she held upside-down, by the bowler's bronze head. When she got close enough, she raised the trophy over her right shoulder and brought it down on Derek's head. There was a thunk as bone met metal. Derek's eyes acquired a momentary dazed look, as if he were remembering some favorite moment from the past. Then he groaned and crumpled to the floor.

"Bastard," Erin said, standing over Derek's body. "Stupid bloody son of a fucking bitch."

She looked at Harry. "Get out of here," she said.

"Will you be okay?"

"Just go."

"But—"

She raised the bowling trophy.

And so Harry got—back down the hall, out the sliding door, across the lawn, and into the woods. He walked quickly. At times, he broke into a trot. It was getting dark and the sun—which by now had broken through the clouds—was sinking, coloring the drops that still clung to leaves. He was lucky he hadn't been killed. After replaying the scene over and over—Derek, Erin, Harry's wallet, the bowling trophy—Harry considered possible future scenarios. Would Derek try to hunt him down? Would Derek even recognize him if they met again? Harry wasn't about to call the cops and it was possible that, after a while, Derek might realize things were genuinely okay. He

26

might forget the whole thing ever happened. But would Erin be alright? Harry couldn't be sure about that. But things weren't exactly rosy for her to begin with. Who knew what went on in that house on a daily basis? Today may have been a mere blip, nowhere near the worst of it. It was even possible that Derek might come around to feeling grateful that Erin brained him. It may have saved him from doing something truly stupid. If Derek was still alive, that is. If he wasn't, well, Erin would have to cook up something to tell the police. Derek was, after all, a drug dealer. Things happened to drug dealers.

Like they happened to drunks. Like what had happened to Harry during his recent sleepover in the new jail, the "glamour slammer" the Seattle papers called it, though there was nothing glamorous Harry could see. He was put in a holding cell with twenty or so other drunks, drug busts, assaulters and batterers, pimps, male prostitutes, and other assorted shit disturbers. He'd sat on the plank bench and tried to remain aloof, which proved more difficult than he thought because a beet-faced, stringy-haired man sporting a tattoo of a skull with a knife rammed through the eye socket had chosen Harry for his personal sounding board.

"What could I do?" the man screamed again and again. "She just wouldn't fucking listen! She just wouldn't fucking listen!"

Each time he said listen, the man pushed Harry hard in the shoulder until Harry's back was slamming against the wall. The man was crazy or high, probably both, and Harry tried to do nothing to upset him. Eventually, a guard noticed what was happening and took the man to another cell. This was a part of Harry's life that his brothers and sister, his friends at work, even Sharon, would never hear anything about. It went into the same classified, top-secret compartment that he planned to file today's little adventure with Erin. And, come to think of it, what would happen the next time he saw Erin? It was bound to happen. On the bus? In the supermarket? He thought about that for a while. Then he understood that he'd treat her the same as anyone else he knew only slightly, the same as someone he'd met during a particularly grueling plane ride, when, at times, the turbulence may have caused them to gasp or shout out or even clutch each other in fear. He'd nod his head. He'd raise an eyebrow and offer the trace of an acknowledging smile. If she smiled back, he might ask about Derek. If not, he'd be on his way.

Inviting Trouble
By Katherine Shirley

She smiled and looked
At the pretty ribbons
Swung the door wide
And with open arms
Welcomed the return
Of your flowered fists

Alma Mater
By Morgan Gallagher

"What is that stench? How can she make such a foul odour?"

Although quiet and polite, Alma's husband could hear the repulsion in her tone, could hear her muscles clenching and her body turning to piano wire as she spoke.

"Don't speak like that in front of Catherine, she can hear you." Acutely aware of his wife's moods, his own words were muted and light, with an attempt at humour. He smiled down at three-week-old Catherine, and rubbed her belly with a light tickle.

"Oh don't do that, she doesn't want a poo-ey hand touching her. Haven't you finished?"

James had indeed finished changing the nappy. Poor Catherine had seemed a little constipated and had squealed and cried and turned bright red as she howled. He'd come home from work to be greeted by the shrieks from the baby carriage in the outer porch whilst Alma had been finishing making dinner in the kitchen.

Alma liked dinner to be on the table in front of him as he walked in the door at 6:15. The screeching from Catherine had been matched by the icy silence from Alma, as he entered at 5:55. Prior to his daughter's birth, he'd have hung around at the train station until he could walk in the door at the correct moment. Now, his desire to hold his daughter in his arms, lift her up and cuddle her, and have that bit more time with her before she was sentenced to the bedroom at 7:15, overrode other considerations.

Alma was furious on two counts. One, he'd come home early and two, dinner wasn't nearly ready. Catherine, it transpired, had been an absolute nightmare all day. Crying, refusing to sleep, refusing to swallow all her bottle, and deliberately vomiting up her milk on her nice, clean clothes.

"Honestly James, she is just like you. She never listens and does exactly what she wants." Alma had stirred the bolognaise sauce she was working on with such speed it slopped out onto the cooker.

"Now look what she's made me do!" Alma took the saucepan off the ring and washed down the cooker top before putting it back on and continuing the frantic swirling.

James had smiled a smile of consolation and comfort, picked up Catherine, and taken her upstairs. Twenty minutes later, with her tummy rubbed and her legs bicycled up and down, she'd finally managed to get rid of the thing that was hurting her and had stopped crying. James had cleaned her up and was just about to put the new nappy on when Alma had arrived to comment on the smell, and to state that dinner was on the table. James thanked his wife and carried Catherine back down the stairs. He placed her in the little Moses basket his mother had given them and watched her look around as he ate his spaghetti.

"I wish you wouldn't keep looking at her like that, she'll get spoiled. She has to learn she's not the centre of the Universe."

James smiled and carried on eating, carried on gazing at his beloved Catherine.

*

The shrieks were ear-piercing. James felt his nerve begin to break. He'd been pacing the living room for over an hour, despite Alma's promises that it wouldn't go on for more than ten minutes. So far he'd kept to his side of the bargain: not to interfere, not to intrude on her authority as the mother. But the feeling of his skin searing off his body and fear knotting up his stomach was becoming impossible to ignore. Every one of Catherine's screams and wails was killing him. He could feel his heart jumping in response. He gave in to his instincts and went upstairs.

Alma was sitting outside the nursery, reading her Women's Weekly. She'd put her chair in front of the door, barring the way. She looked up at him as he emerged onto the landing. Her eyes rolled and the magazine was put down with a huff.

"Oh for goodness sake, James! She's perfectly all right!"

"She doesn't sound all right." He'd had to raise his voice to be heard above the cries.

"She is warm, well-fed, safe, and comfortable. I double filled her bottle to get her through the night and her nappy is dry. There is nothing wrong with her."

"She's lonely!" His voice raised until it was almost matching Alma's extortions.

"She's in a TEMPER. You don't propose to raise a spoilt brat, do you?"

"She's six months old, how can she be spoiled?"

"Easily, with you around. Always picking her up, cuddling her, telling her what a good girl she is. Always rushing to her for the slightest whimper. You've caused this!"

James stared at his wife. The schism that existed in their world had never seemed so great, so profound.

"How can you bear to hear her in pain like this?"

"She is not in pain. She's in a temper, and heaven knows if we don't control it now, we'll have worse to come." Alma seemed not to hear the pain in James's voice. "She has to learn to sleep, and this is how she'll do it. Not by being mollycoddled by you."

Alma picked the magazine back up and purposely stared at the pages. James had been dismissed. Short of physically pushing her out of the chair to get to the nursery, there was nothing he could do. He stormed back down the stairs, pulled his coat off the hook, and left.

"Another night at the pub whilst I do the hard work," Alma spoke out loud, as if addressing the baby through the door.

"Now see what you have done...."

*

James opened the door at 6:13. "I'm home!"

Alma smiled her greeting, and her thanks as she placed the dinner out on the table.

"Smells good!" said James as he hung up his coat. "I'll just wash my hands." He ducked into the downstairs toilet that Alma had had installed under the stairs. She was immensely pleased with this civilized addition to the house. James would have preferred... well, quite a lot of things, actually, but it was keeping Alma happy.

Alma was settling Catherine into the high chair as he seated himself. Beef Cobbler was one of his favourites; once again, Alma was showing her thanks for him giving in on the extension.

"Well, how have my girls been today?"

Frost formed in the air as Alma launched into her tirade of how trying her day had been. James tried to tune it out and concentrate on Catherine, who was playing with a rattle he'd bought for her, but it was difficult.

"... And then she spit up all over her new bib. I'd starched it, too, when I ironed it, and she got bits in the little embroidery roses. I'll never get them looking that good again...."

"Tut," said James quietly. He winked at Catherine. Alma didn't pause for breath.

"... so I tried the new banana one, and she spat that out, too. I mean, what child doesn't like mashed banana? It took me an hour to get that jar into her. I was exhausted by the time for her nap, and then she threw up all over her clean bedding, so I had to re-feed her and do the bed linen...."

James spooned down his dinner, trying to juggle his attention between the women in his life. Alma would erupt if she felt she wasn't getting enough, or that Catherine was getting too much. All he wanted was to beam and smile at Catherine, and talk to her in little whispers and tickle her until she started to hiccup with laughter. He nodded and smiled at Alma enough times to keep her mollified whilst giving Catherine his secret smile and pulling faces that Alma couldn't see. Catherine giggled. Alma droned on....

"Claire was round, and she said little Emily never spits out her food, and every scrap is taken from the jar... and heaven knows Emily doesn't manage to stink out the room every time she breathes...."

Catherine dropped the rattle on the floor as she squealed in laughter.

"That's it, that's the third time today."

As James had leaned down to pick up the rattle, Alma swooped up Catherine. A sharp slap and a sharper cry filled the air, and James's heart.

"Never, never, never do that again." On each 'never,' Alma slapped the back of Catherine's hand, hard. Catherine's howls became screams as Alma whisked her up the stairs. "When will you learn?"

James looked at his beef congealing into the gravy and listened to the uproar upstairs as Catherine was stripped of her clothes, pushed and pulled into a sleep suit, and the door firmly closed on her cries. By the time Alma came back downstairs, he was in the pub.

*

"There, who is a pretty girl, then?" James finished buttoning Catherine's coat and stood up to look at her. How could she be so grown up? She looked tiny and vulnerable in her school uniform, which – like all first school uniforms – was too big for her. Catherine looked up at her Daddy with adoring eyes and smiled.

"Will I do then, Daddy?"

James laughed and was just about to speak when Alma came

rushing into the hall.

"Oh, for goodness sake, aren't you ready yet? We'll be late. Catherine, what is that bird's nest on top of your head? You don't think it's a hairstyle, do you?" She shot James the look, the one that made it clear that Daddy was an idiot and how could he call that pigtails? James ignored her and leaned down to try and adjust the approved school ribbons.

"Oh don't make it worse!" Alma slapped James's hand out of the way, pulling the ribbons off. Cathy squealed.

"Oh be quiet, I didn't hurt you." She unpicked the pigtails and pulled a brush through, starting again in double quick time. As she twisted the first layer in deeply, pulling the hair tightly into the scalp, Cathy squealed again. Alma slapped her bare legs with the palm of her hand.

"Don't argue back. I've told you, you have to suffer for beauty; you better get used to it now. I'm not having everyone looking down on us as your hair falls out halfway through the day. I've told you, you have to finish the day as neat as you start it. Is that clear?"

Cathy nodded, her eyes brimming with tears. James turned away, breathing deeply.

"There, that's much better. Make sure the ribbons don't come out, won't you, sweetheart?" Alma dropped down to Cathy's height.

"You know Mummy loves you, don't you, darling? I just want the best for you." James turned back to look at his girls. Tears were brimming in Alma's eyes and her voice was choked. James patted her on the shoulder.

"She'll do her best, won't you, Cathy?"

"There's no 'Cathy' in this house, is there, Catherine...?" Alma's tone had returned to its usual cadence of disapproval and frustration.

"No, Mummy, only a Catherine," Cathy sing-songed back to her.

"And don't you forget that at school today. If the girls call you Cathy, you tell them politely and nicely that your name is CATH-ER-INE. Is that clear?"

"Yes, Mummy."

"Good girl. Well then, let's get going, we can't be late!"

Alma had already instructed James that he was not to get out of the car at the school gates.

"None of the other fathers even turn up. Of course, I'd need my own car to be able drop her off myself."

"We can't afford another car and the school fees. The uniform alone cost enough to buy you a little banger."

"A banger! You'd let your wife drive a second-hand car? Well, that shouldn't surprise me...."

James had taken in a deep breath and counted to twenty. Once, he'd only needed to count to ten. He had wondered what would happen if he ever needed to get to thirty....

She looked so small and fragile as Alma led her across the school yard to the lines of children waiting patiently. The nuns looked so tall in their habits, so severe. He hated that Alma had won this battle; every instinct in him wanted him to get out of the car, gather his little treasure up in his arms, and take her away as quickly as he could. With a final instruction of some sort, Alma let go of her hand and backed off to hover with the ring of mothers looking on anxiously. Alma wasn't anxious. She beamed with pride and happiness at the sight of her Catherine in the long line of silent little girls, who looked as if they had been made from a biscuit cutter; with their identical hats, blazers, satchels, and pigtails. The nun on the top step of the school doorway rang a large hand-bell she carried. The lines started to move into the school, older girls first.

James watched as his perfect child, his little girl, his lover of cuddles and tickles, stood the longest and marched in last: the baby class.

He gunned the car up to life. The revving disturbed the silence that had fallen on the playground as the mothers had nodded and smiled to each other. Alma's eyebrows rose up and she shot him another icy gaze. He ignored it, and when she finally got into the car, he wrecked the gears as he tried to drive off quickly. The car shuddered and stalled. He jabbed the pedal down and pulled the key around hard.

"Careful. You don't want to flood the engine."

He remained silent as he slowly started to count to fifty.

*

"Mum, no one else wears pigtails in my class."

"If everyone in your class jumped off a cliff, would you follow?" Alma continued to stitch the starched ribbons with their perfect bows onto Catherine's hair.

34

"No, Mummy."

"Exactly." Alma snipped off the thread. "There, that will survive gym class. Now, let's check your bag."

Catherine opened up her school bag, which had been her Christmas present. It was gleaming soft tan leather with her initials in gold under the lock. Alma had painted over the brass lock in clear nail varnish to ensure that her clumsy daughter didn't scratch the plate with the key. The books and tools of school were laid out neatly, every text book and jotter double-lined in brown wrapping paper. Alma had been shocked when the nuns had started to allow wrapping in coloured wrapping paper, and the subsequent competition that had then begun to see who had the most stylish covers had irritated her no end.

"I'm not spending money on fancy wrapping paper! Your father works hard enough as it is, it's not fair to him. You shouldn't pester him so... it'll be the death of him!"

Catherine had sighed as she put away the bright red paper her dad had brought home for her, and rewrapped her math book with the brown paper wrapping. Dad, hiding behind his newspaper, had grumped and rustled the pages.

"Don't you have something better to do?" Alma's tone had pierced through the newsprint. Dad had got up and gone to his shed, taking his paper with him.

"Not that he ever does anything useful down there...."

Catherine had watched her father walk down the path with a queer sense of pain in her heart. She wasn't allowed in the shed... it wasn't suitable for a young girl to see all that rubbish and clutter lying around. The door had banged shut and Catherine had known he would switch on Radio 4 and light up. He wasn't allowed to smoke in the house, it was smelly and unhygienic; her mother hated that he'd started to smoke.

"Did you hear what I said?"

Catherine dragged her attention back to her mother, who had finished counting off the books and checking the homework schedule.

"How you manage to pay attention in class, I do not know!"

Catherine knew. Anything was better than the leather belt the nuns used, and the shame of being made to kneel in front of the blackboard, your knees aching from the hard wood as you were made to recite ten Holy Marys and ask for forgiveness. Catherine had only been subjected to the kneeling once; once was enough. Not like poor Teresa Reddy, whose hair always came loose, who dropped things, and who was never quite sure of what she should be doing. Teresa had patches in her blazer as it was a hand-me-down, and her shoes were scuffed. Mum tutted every time she saw Teresa and said that the school standards had dropped. Teresa's father was the school caretaker and Alma was furious that he got a reduction on the fees. Teresa spent so much time on her knees in front of the blackboard, her back to the class, that the others teased her she was going to be a nun.

Catherine had never wanted that said to her, and so she had never, ever missed the teacher speaking to her again. Her mother continued to prattle as they went through the pre-school ritual.

"And I want to see an improvement in your spelling today. Sister Mary Gabriel said you got one wrong yesterday."

Catherine blushed. "Yes, Mum."

"Don't take that insolent tone with me." Alma pulled up Catherine's chin so they were looking into each other's eyes.

"I only push you as I want the best for you, sweetheart." Alma's eyes misted over, her voice wavered. "I just want the best for you, darling. I want you to have everything I never had. I want you to shine." A tear dripped out of the corner of Alma's eye. Catherine's eyes misted over.

"Oh please, Mummy, don't cry! I'll get all my spelling right, I promise."

"That's a good girl." Alma took a handkerchief out of her cardigan pocket, wiping first her own eyes, then Catherine's.

"I know you're a good girl at heart, you just need to learn to listen." Alma smiled brightly. "Now, look at your lunch!"

Catherine looked at the little Tupperware box.

"What is it, Mummy?"

"Look and see! I've worked extra hard!"

Catherine swallowed the sigh. Alma had taught Catherine to swallow sighs well.

She clicked open the box. Inside were three little boxes. She put the big box down on the hall table. The first little box contained a sliced apple.

"I've dipped them in lemon juice to keep them from growing

36

brown. And lemon dissolves fat!"

Catherine smiled, swallowing hard.

The second box contained some cottage cheese with green bits on it.

"That's dill. It helps the digestion!"

Catherine smiled and swallowed again.

The third box contained grated carrots with brown lumps.

"That's the big surprise. I know the recipe said to use currants, but dried fruit like that is just a parcel of sugar. So those are little lumps of prune, to help keep you regular."

Catherine looked at her Mummy and smiled.

"Thank you so much."

Alma beamed at her.

"That's okay, darling. Anything for you, to keep you healthy and happy. We can't have you getting any fatter, can we...?"

Catherine carefully packed her bag and put her water bottle in the pocket of her school overcoat.

Alma fussed them into the car and drove them off to the school gates. They were in Daddy's big car, as Mum had said he could only smoke in the little second-hand one. No point in smoking out a new car: it just lost more value.

As Alma watched Catherine disappear into the school gate she spoke out loud into the empty car.

"Try and swap any of that for the crap the other girls have!"

*

"Why can't we go and visit Daddy's grave, Mummy?"

"It makes you too upset. You cry, and it's pointless."

"But Mum, I'd like...."

"THAT IS ENOUGH. Do you not think I work my fingers to the bone for you as it is? It's costing a fortune to keep you in that school and I've had enough of this. A grateful daughter would be making her mother a cup of tea now, not screeching on about how UNFAIR LIFE IS. LIFE IS UNFAIR, CATHERINE, how many times have I told you about that? It's not as if...."

Catherine sat very still. If she could just make herself as small and still as possible, whilst still looking attentive....

"And don't you dare give me that look! Don't you DARE look at me like that! What have I ever done to deserve your cheek, and your stubbornness? No wonder you put your father in his grave... without pestering him there as well!"

Catherine sent herself to her room where she swallowed it all down with the chocolate she'd stolen from the local shop.

*

"I just don't see how you can do it. I just don't know how you can get through the day, knowing you look like this."

Catherine was laid out on her mother's lap. A cushion from the couch was on her mother's lap and Catherine's head was on the cushion. They'd already done the left side of her face, and thus they'd moved to the other end of the couch so the right side of Catherine's face could be presented to her mother, whilst she, Catherine, kept her attention glued to Top of the Pops on the television in the far corner. Alma had laid out her instruments on a cushion beside her: a needle kit, tweezers, a match for sterilizing, and cotton balls.

Catherine was trying to listen to David Cassidy as her mother dug into her ears.

"How you do not know how dirty you are is beyond me... it's not like I don't make you wash...."

The needle was being pricked into her ear. Catherine flinched.

"I've told you not to move. I don't want to make a red mark. I never make a red mark."

Catherine remained still.

Alma's nails dug into the skin on the inside of Catherine's ears.

"Oh my god! LOOK AT IT. It's huge!"

Alma continued to press down.

"Oh, and the smell...."

Alma made as if to gag.

Catherine kept staring at David Cassidy's face, although she'd lost the ability to hear the words. His mouth kept moving, his eyes kept shining, and his hair kept gleaming. Catherine filled in the words under her breath.

"Look at it." Alma's voice had dipped low to concern and care as she leaned her hand over into Catherine's vision.

On Alma's impeccable nail, in a long squirm of worm, was the blackhead that had been squeezed out of Catherine's inner ear. It was thick and whitish.

"Just look at THAT!"

Alma had used the needle to zero in on the round black plug at the end of the string of sebum.

"Look at that dirt. That's what people can see when they stand next to you. How can you bear it? You might not be able to see into your ears, but other people can. What will they think of me, you being out in this sort of state?"

Catherine apologized for her failings. Alma bit her tongue and continued the attack on Catherine's face, moving to her nose and forehead.

What was the point? The child never listened. Had no pride. She was just wasting her breath. She dug the needle back in to the annoying pore at the end of Catherine's nose that would not close, no matter what she painted on it. Catherine closed her eyes and counted to twenty.

*

"I'm so happy you could come this evening, it's been such a relief to talk to fellow grown-ups. More wine...?"

Monica giggled as Alma filled up her glass. George offered his glass up.

"And how is the practice going, George? Settling in?"

"Oh yes, very well. They're a good bunch, I was lucky to get the partnership." George quaffed the wine. "How's that delightful young girl of yours?"

Alma's face fell a little. Monica looked over in concern.

"I'm so glad you asked. It's been difficult...." Alma's voice wavered and a tear slid out of her eye. Monica leaned over and patted her on the shoulder whilst George concentrated on his wine glass.

His retreat was firmly halted, as Alma launched at him.

"I did want to speak to you, George, if you could speak to her... as you are a doctor...?"

George stared, a little open-mouthed, and Monica pincered in.

"I did say to you, George, how worried Alma is...?"

George stared at his joint doom and nodded, trying to move sideways again.

"It's just as I told you, Monica dearest, if Alma is that worried, she should see her own GP and have Catherine referred to a dietician... I can't...."

Alma looked as if she was going to burst into tears but was

containing it, just. Monica launched full frontal.

"Oh think of the shame, George! Everyone would know about it. It would be the gossip of the school! Alma doesn't deserve that, especially since she's sacrificed so much for Catherine."

Alma made another effort to contain her crying. A single tear slid from her left eye. George watched her dab at it with her napkin.

"Oh very well, I'll have a word with her, if you like."

"Oh thank you, George, I'm so grateful. Brandy?"

George drank two down in quick succession. How to get out of this....

The nightmare unfolded with meticulous planning. They retired to the living room to find a set of scales had already been placed out. George tried to settle on the arm chair, had a chair even been made more uncomfortable? Alma filled up his brandy glass as she settled into her own chair. Monica sat beside her, hugging her Bailey's Irish Cream. George felt he might suffocate.

In front of her, Alma held a chart.

"I only asked you tonight as she had been doing quite well. She lost two pounds the week before last and three the week before that," her light and hopeful tones slowed and dropped to a pained whisper, "but only one pound last week." Alma looked at George as if she were a half-drowned kitten and he the rescue services. "I felt a little encouragement from you would help so much. Keep her on the right track."

George swallowed down the brandy, not tasting it. Jesus, he needed to get out of here.

Catherine, who had been called to attend downstairs as they'd settled into the living room, came in.

George's heart leaped. She was such a timid little thing. She'd had her bath whilst they'd eaten and was wrapped up in her winceyette pyjamas and dressing gown. Her eyes stared at him as she realised the room held others. She was the same age as their Timothy; and a chubbier, more unnoticeable thirteen-year-old could not be found. George had always felt, however, that she would be the beauty of the family once she'd stretched. Her fine skin and clear eyes were perfect, her cheeks had a sharp slant, and there was a length of bone waiting to blossom out of her in good time. Under the layer of puppy fat, an elegant and graceful young woman was waiting to emerge. George felt his ears flush. How had he got roped into this?

"Catherine, dearest, Monica and George have asked to be able to support you in our... little struggle...."

Catherine looked at her mother the way a mouse might look at an owl. George swallowed down the brandy, finishing the glass.

He wasn't sure who was more miserable, himself or the ghastly-fated Catherine. Alma, her clip board and her chart in hand, had instructed the teenager to stand on the scales. Catherine looked frozen, her hands on the belt of her dressing gown. Alma observed the panic and tut-tutted it.

"Catherine dear, you know George is a doctor! And it's not as if Monica hasn't changed your nappy once or twice. Don't be so dramatic, you've not got anything we've not seen before."

Monica giggled. George heard the note of hysteria. Oh lord, let this be over.

"Don't make her take her gown off if she doesn't want to, Alma." There, he'd found his voice.

"Don't be silly, George. She has to wear the same clothes every time. She knows that." Towards George, Alma's voice was warm and comforting. It sharpened and thinned when addressed to Catherine. "Take off your dressing gown and get on the scales."

George watched, aghast, as the child fumbled and blushed and then went white. She dropped the gown on the floor and stood on the scales. She was lumpier, and redder, under the gown. She looked at the floor and crossed her arms in front of herself.

"Eyes up and arms down, Catherine."

Catherine did what she was told, automatically. George saw the flame blaze across her cheeks. His own gaze dropped to his shoes.

Monica giggled.

Alma stood up and went over to the scales. "Well that's...." her voice stopped. George felt his heart racing and his pulse skip a beat.

"You've put on THREE pounds!"

What George remembered most about what followed was how powerless he had felt. It niggled him for years that he should have spoken up, or at the very least, walked out. But somehow, in the face of Alma's shouting, and pleading with him and Monica to get through to the child, what he'd actually done was agree that putting on weight was very dangerous, that it put a strain on the heart and yes, her mother was right, no decent man would look at her whilst she was fat.

His patients gained from the horror of what he took part in that night. He always treated a woman complaining about weight, either for themselves, or their child or husband, extremely sympathetically. However, he could never forgive himself for the tirade that had been opened up on that poor child's head, and how he'd sat back and watched her shake.

For Catherine's part the night was branded into her soul. She lay in bed and wept silent tears. At no point had she felt able to mention to her mother, remind her mother, that her period had started that morning, and she was 'allowed' the benefit of water retention on those days. Alma had hoped that there wouldn't be a little spike in that week, just no actual weight lost... which is what Catherine fervently wished for when she was being weighed whilst bleeding. She'd been too horrified at having to take off her dressing gown in front of everyone. Terrified the bulge of her sanitary towel would be seen through her pyjamas. The thought of speaking up and asking for the circumstances to be taken into account... for saying anything that might have caused her mother to refer to what was going on in her body in front of the others, the man....

That night she bled heavily into the sheets. Faced with her ruin in the morning, she balled up the mess and pushed the sheets under her bed. She remade the bed with clean sheets.

It was four months before Alma found the sheets. Catherine was having a sleep over with Clare and Emily, and Alma decided to clean out the bedroom, see what secrets were being hidden. She found the balled up sheets, surrounded by empty chocolate and sweet wrappers. She burned the sheets and cleaned out the entire bedroom of its shameful treasures.

Nothing was said but sweet wrappers and chocolate crumbs were never found in the room again.

*

"But Mum, I don't like him."

Alma sighed, long and deep.

"I know you are jealous of him. I know you like having me all to yourself. It's natural to be unsure of a new... Father."

42

"He is not my father!" Catherine could not swallow that down.

"He is my husband, and you will respect him."

Catherine's head dropped down and she stared at her shoes. Alma felt the defiance radiate out in waves. She decided 'softly softly' was the better option here.

"Catherine, darling." Her hand reached out and lifted up her daughter's chin, pulling her into contact with her. Alma's eyes swam with unshed tears, her voice trembled in longing and hurt.

"Please darling. Don't grudge me a little happiness. Andrew is a wonderful man and he makes me happy. He makes you happy too, who do you think pays for your riding lessons?"

Tears spilled out of Catherine's eyes.

"He cares very much for you. He bought you that lovely new bike, so you can get to the stables. I'm sure, in time, you'll see how much he cares for you."

Catherine already knew how much Andrew cared for her. As she looked up at her mother's tears she knew she couldn't say any more: it would hurt Alma too much.

She'd just have to put up with it, at least until she managed to leave home.

Alma dried both their tears. She hugged Catherine a little, then pulled back.

"Catherine! Have you felt how fat your back feels?"

Catherine stared at her mother, the tears frozen in and locked down.

"Come upstairs, right now. I want to see what you weigh."

Alma physically pulled her up the stairs by the hand, as if she was a child. She was stripped to her underwear and weighed.

In the rage that followed, in the awful waves of screeching and pleading, begging and fury that spilled out from Alma's mouth... in the tirade about how she was a selfish, ungrateful child, with no self-respect and no understanding of the world... Catherine really only noticed one thing. That Andrew had slipped upstairs and was standing at the bathroom doorway, peeping in, whilst Alma flew around her, arms flailing and fingers pointing. Standing, staring at her in her underwear, with that look upon his face: the look her mother never saw. She closed her eyes and wished herself far, far away, but Alma's voice would not let her go.

"AND HOW DO YOU THINK ANY DECENT MAN WILL EVER FANCY YOU IN THAT STATE! You will NEVER get a boyfriend; no one will EVER find you attractive."

Catherine could only hope.

*

The entire office was on edge, waiting for the manager's door to open back up. Seeing two police officers come into the building and then go into her office had set everyone's tongues wagging. Who was in trouble? Was something wrong? Three people had already phoned home to see if there was a problem there.

No one had been expecting it to be about Big Cathy. She'd carried on ignoring everything as she typed away in her little booth.

Nothing was ever about Big Cathy.

But it was Cathy who had been called in when the door opened again. Cathy who emerged ten minutes later, pale and shaking, to be led to a police car by the female officer. Jill, the manager, had already packed up her handbag and held her coat out to her. Cathy had nodded her thanks and then left, silent as ever.

The ride to the hospital was somewhat surreal. All she could really hear was the news that Andrew was dead. The officers had said something about her mother, a lot about her mother, but it didn't make any sense to her. All she could feel, all she could know, was that Andrew was dead.

She stood in the ICU, at the bottom of her mother's bed. Wires, lines, leads, and dressings covered her mother's body. Her legs were in traction, as was one arm. The doctor pulled her to one side, into an office, to explain it all again. He was beginning to wonder if this girl was a little slow, a little "special."

He again took her through the catalogue of injuries. That the speed with which the emergency services had got to the crash site was the only thing that had saved her mother's life.

That her father had died instantly and therefore had felt no pain.

"He's not my father." It was the only thing she kept saying, really. Did she have a guardian somewhere, someone legally responsible for her?

Catherine just looked at him again, in complete silence. When he ran out of things to say about her mother's prognosis, she nodded and left without speaking.

The law firm that handled all her step-father's affairs managed everything very smoothly. She was very happy with them. No one

44

was surprised that Andrew had left everything to Catherine: he'd adored her after all. Alma would have argued, no doubt, had she been able to.

Whilst it had looked as if intensive physical therapy might improve Alma's mental state, a year after the accident Catherine was appointed legal guardian of her mother's affairs. There had only been one point of disagreement between the law firm and Catherine. They had resisted her impulse to care full-time for her mother. Her physical disabilities were so profound, her mental state so damaged... could she not see that a high-quality care facility would be better for Alma, if not Catherine? A young woman in her twenties should not have to care full time for someone unable to speak or communicate in anyway. Someone who required a machine to breathe. Someone who was doubly incontinent and required a tube to feed.

Someone who may live another five, ten, or even twenty years, with enough ongoing care.

She had won her argument and had the dining room converted into a room capable of supporting her mother's medical needs. She spent many hours in the hospital, making sure Alma had the support she needed to be well enough physically to be sent home. The physiotherapist that had been employed to encourage Alma to try and talk, to try and communicate somehow, felt that Cathy was a saint. Alma must have been a wonderful mother for Cathy to be so devoted to her. She'd always been there, no matter what. Holding her mother's hands down when she spasmed, wiping the tears of frustration from her eyes. No one could understand Alma the way her daughter did, and it was obvious that Alma felt the same way. Whenever anyone spoke Cathy's name out loud, Alma's face trembled. It was heartening to see such mutual love: somewhere deep down in the scar tissue the accident had left in Alma's brain, she still knew her daughter.

Cathy herself had obviously struggled at times. She'd resigned from her job and had lost a great deal of weight. The physio had urged her to take better care of herself: if she got ill, who was going to care for her mother? In the end, the physio had agreed with everyone else and signed Alma out to her daughter's devoted care. Although the burden of caring for her mother would be great, the girl deserved to have her mother with her as long as she could, didn't she?

She said as much to the ambulance drivers when they drove

away from delivering Alma to Cathy's care. It had taken two hours to transfer her the three miles from the hospital and get everything set up. The driver commented on how nice and supportive the young girl had been, and how nice it was to see someone take on caring for someone. The driver spoke out what everyone always thought after seeing Cathy care for Alma:

"She must have been one hell of a mother."

Cathy watched the ambulance leave the driveway. She pressed a button and the gates closed and locked automatically. She switched the outside lights off.

Opening her mother's room, the smell hit her first. Alma had voided her bowels. Cathy looked at her, smiled, and pulled on a set of disposable plastic gloves.

"My my, what a terrible stench. Who could have made such a foul smell...? Did you deliberately wait until the ambulance crew had left...?" Cathy made a gagging noise as she pulled back the covers. Alma's cheeks flamed red.

"Honestly, Mother, what have you been eating? You smell like a sewer. Never mind, we'll soon fix that." Cathy cleaned her up quickly, using the hoist to lift up her legs as she slipped a clean adult nappy under her bottom. All the time she explained to Alma what she was doing, what a hard and tiresome task it was, how shocking Alma's body looked with its scars and broken bone ridges.

"Good thing no one will ever see those useless legs again, Mother, that's a blessing at least."

She washed Alma's face with a cold flannel and brushed through her hair, pulling out the tangles before twisting it into two tight pigtails.

"Cold water is so good for closing the pores, isn't it mother? I'll get some of that moisturiser you like tomorrow, from the chemist. Must try and keep your skin from aging so badly. You have a shocking amount of lines and wrinkles. Monica and George are coming to see you tomorrow. I'll make sure you're looking your best, don't worry. Not a hair will be out of place."

She checked the machines, double-checked the tubes and dressings on Alma's arms, smoothed down the linen coverlet.

"I expect you're very tired after the ride in the ambulance. Best get to sleep now, Mother, conserve your strength. I know it's early but you have to get your rest. I had the curtains lined with blackout material you know, just like my bedroom. So nothing can disturb the

46

dark, nothing to keep you awake. You'll be fine Mother, just fine. Routine, that's the key: routine and order. That will make everything all right. You taught me well."

Cathy turned and left the room, not looking back as she turned off the light and closed the door.

In the glow of the beeping machines, tears slid from Alma's eyes.

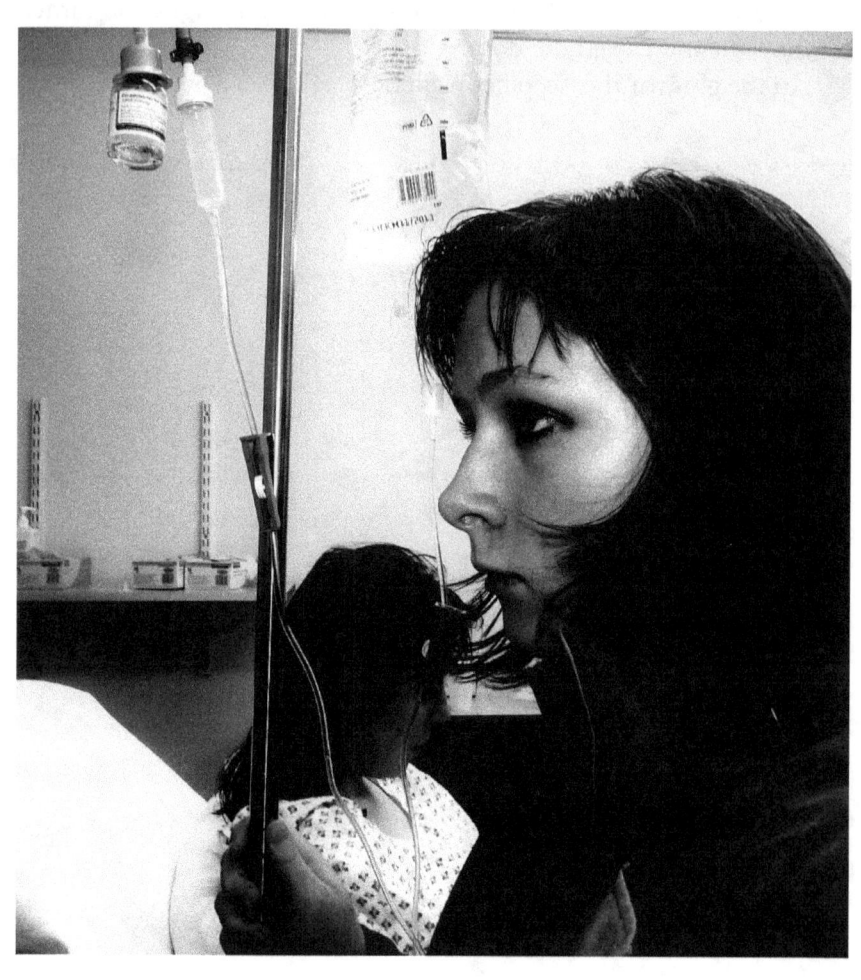

Least Said Soonest Better
Eleanor Leonne Bennett

Damaged Goods
By henry 7. reneau, jr.

a ripped box leaking foam packaging peanuts,
a mind stamped: damaged in transit

& manhandled by childhood trauma—
stretching her guts & ass & hooking

the anchor of her heart
into something deep & treacherous,

a naïve love looking up into betrayal—
because suffering is her soul biography & not all

has been written.
whip-crack suffering justifies her rage—

there is nothing but howling wind and solitary birds—
a wounded confidence

already veined with scars
& a belief, now, that all men are dogs.

her conviction assuming the blame—the buck—
confounding her sexuality

& blessing her with a mouth doomed to be slapped
& punched; do not fold, spindle, or mutilate

& black skid-marks defacing a torn & crumpled letter,
(photograph enclosed) passed hand to hand to hand

as a steel door slams on her anger & shame for being born
a girl amongst sharks (jaws agape

& slicing from the dark)—an offering—a piece of herself
for a piece of a holocaust moment.

Anger Paintings
By Frances Pauli

Marks on my throat
From thick fingers
Blue-black, golden pressure points,
Anger paintings.
The rage of your tears as I
Comfort you.

I comfort you.

Screaming drunk outside
The little tent,
Puking,
Face down in the Oregon grape, slick with
Your toxic alcohol
As you apologize, not for hurting.

So sorry for being ill,
Your puking far less hostile,
Less offending
Than the purpled existence
Of your shining, puffing
Face in candlelight.

A Slap In The Face
By Katherine Shirley

I saw it in a movie once
The way she did nothing
Just stood there and took it
Spoke to me

Face snapped to one side
In a stylish parody of pain
Then the picture turned
Until the music tasted
Sour in my mouth

Stubborn defiance in her gaze
Told the wrong story
I wanted to shout
Wave my arms at the screen
Wanted to make her hear me

Don't look at him!
My mind was screaming
Keep your head down!
Don't be stupid!

There is nothing heroic
In taking the second blow
I was right
By the time he raised his fist
To strike again
The camera was looking away

Object Obsession
By Enigma

What have I become?
I don't want to be a whore...
Why do I detest myself?
I don't want to do it anymore....

It comes so easily
And he finishes off,
then the attention
he gives
is pretty much
cut off

I am just a body type,
conveniently placed
To satisfy lust
why do I do it with haste?

there's nothing personal
nothing to trust
when your body
is just a wanted object
to satisfy lust

The Doll
By Brenda L Turner

As soon as she and her husband, Mark, arrived, Megan noticed her. Reminding her of an exotic porcelain doll with ebony hair cascading down her back, jeweled barrettes pinning back her bangs to enhance her smoky emerald eyes, deep purple off the shoulder cocktail dress accentuating her perfect hourglass figure, the woman was mesmerizing. If Megan didn't know any better, she'd have thought this woman was a real life enchantress from a fairytale.

"This is Jasmine, my wife," Paul, Mark's colleague, introduced the woman to them. As the last guests arrived, because she had an extraordinary talent to impress, Jasmine was sent away by Paul to play hostess. Always smiling, constantly refilling champagne glasses, making polite conversation, and always giving Paul all the credit instead of taking any herself, Jasmine was the exact opposite of Paul, who reminded Megan of a puffed up peacock with his arrogance. It didn't take her long to realize that Jasmine was only a toy to him, a beautiful doll; he had even called her his doll on several occasions throughout the night. At first, Megan had seen it as a term of endearment, but as the evening wore on and no hint of affection was bestowed between the couple, she realized it was more of a reminder for Jasmine of her role as Paul's wife.

Jasmine played her role both as hostess and Paul's doll to perfection until dinner was served. It was then Megan noticed Jasmine very discreetly kick her five-inch stilettos off her feet under the table once she was finally seated. Megan also noticed Paul whisper something to his wife who immediately slipped the shoes back on. She quickly gave Jasmine a look of sympathy, and Jasmine smiled, whispering a quick, "Thank you." The look Paul gave Megan made her fear what consequences Jasmine might be dealt. The entire atmosphere had transformed from relaxed and carefree before dinner to the exact opposite afterward, and the party ended abruptly with Paul's announcement of an "unexpected family problem."

Megan and Mark had been among the last to leave. As they were leaving, Megan gave Jasmine a friendly hug, complimenting her on her incredible skill as a hostess when she caught the glimpse of possessive rage in Paul's eyes. A rage she knew all too well from having grown up with an abusive father.

On the drive home, Megan asked her husband about Paul. "Mark, do you ever notice how Paul treats Jasmine? Like she's on display?" Mark just shook his head. "They've been like that since I've known them; Paul loves his wife. He does so much for her – takes her on cruises, trips to Hawaii and Europe, buys her all kinds of jewelry. They love each other. Don't worry about it. It's nothing. He's not your father. Jasmine is perfectly fine."

Meanwhile, back at Paul's house, Jasmine was crying, sitting on the floor of her shower. Paul had finally left after verbally attacking her about the shoe incident, her dress being too revealing, and her supposed flirting. The verbal attacks gave way to physical assaults that left bruises and cuts on Jasmine, who had been pushed against the wall and then to the floor. Paul finally grabbed Jasmine's hair and dragged her into the bedroom. Pushing her onto the bed, Paul forced himself on her, "to teach her a lesson about being a slut." When he finished, he got up, took a shower, and coming back into the bedroom, told Jasmine, "Get cleaned up and put ice on those bruises. I'm going to see Amber. She lets me do whatever I want to her and never complains. She's nothing like you." Amber was a dancer at The Dollhouse who Paul favored because of her submission to Paul's every sexual whim, unlike Jasmine who loathed even the thought of Paul touching her.

As soon as Paul was gone, Jasmine dragged herself into the shower. She had been in there an hour, sitting on the floor of the tub, letting the hot water wash away her tears – tears for the happiness and freedom she had lost years ago.

Thinking back to their whirlwind romance, Jasmine remembered Paul as her real life Prince Charming. Tall, dark, and handsome with his 6'4" athletic build, mocha hair, and storm cloud gray eyes, he had been a successful criminal defense attorney who had both an adventurous and a charming side. He had both intimidated and intrigued Jasmine, and he chose her – a starving actress moonlighting as a bartender at an upscale bar in upper Manhattan – over every other woman in the bar that first night.

The moment he walked into the bar that night, all eyes were on him; he had his choice of women. As he sat at the end of the bar, he caught Jasmine's eyes, smiled, and waved her over.

"Hi, beautiful. What's your name?"

"Jasmine," she said shyly. No one had ever called her beautiful the way he had.

"Well, Jasmine, I'm Paul. We would like four shots of Grey Goose, chilled glasses."

At his request, Jasmine served Paul and his friends drinks the rest of the night, receiving a substantial tip at closing. Also, Paul waited to leave until the end of Jasmine's shift, escorted her to her car, and took her out to breakfast, catching her heart with his gentlemanly manner. The night ended with a kiss and the start of a promising relationship.

It had been a romance that swept Jasmine off her feet from the very beginning. Paul spoiled her with dozens of roses, jewelry, and trips to the Caribbean.

"I feel so safe in your arms," Jasmine told him one night.

"I promise you will always be safe with me, Babydoll. I love you and will always protect you," Paul told her, holding her tightly. The prince she had dreamed about since first reading Cinderella had captured her, asked her to marry him, and promised to love her forever. The wedding was out of a fairytale, and that day was the day she knew she would live happily ever after. The honeymoon was even more amazing. He surprised her with a trip to Paris – a city she'd always dreamed of visiting. The next two weeks were heavenly – candlelit dinners, walks through the city, coffee at little street cafes, a visit to the Eiffel tower. She wanted to freeze time just to stay there in that place, in those moments, forever and ever.

To her dismay it ended too soon, but Paul had another surprise when they got home - a two-story townhouse across the street from Central Park. It had a kitchen with a breakfast nook, a fireplace, and a spiral staircase. Upstairs, the master bedroom had a majestic feel with its deep cherry furniture, magnificent canopy bed, and a window overlooking the park. The deep purple color scheme enhanced the royal atmosphere. A Jacuzzi tub surrounded by Jasmine's favorite lavender and vanilla scented bath salts, oils, and candles sat in a corner of the master bath. It was everything Jasmine had ever wanted.

Jasmine's mind wandered to the first night in their new place. She had soaked in the most luxurious bubble bath in her life and dressed in a real silk slip that felt incredibly soft against her skin. When she had walked down the stairs to surprise Paul, though, his reaction had been unexpected.

"Jasmine, what do you think you're doing?" he demanded.

"What do you mean? I was surprising you. I thought you'd find it sexy," Jasmine answered, looking down and playing with the hem of her slip.

"Sexy? You come down barely dressed, knowing the blinds stay open til bedtime, and you think it's sexy? I hate to tell you, Doll, but it's slutty, not sexy. Now go back upstairs like my good little girl; I'll be up in a minute." That was the night her fairytale began to unravel.

Paul's verbal attacks soon turned into physical assaults. One particular night after Jasmine had spent a lovely afternoon with an old friend, she arrived home to find an especially enraged Paul, who threw stuff at her. She ended up in the hospital needing stitches after a wineglass Paul threw hit her in the forehead, just missing her eye. That same night, Paul began demanding make-up sex after their fights instead of the ritual apologies, begging for forgiveness, and gift buying. Jasmine had tried resisting to no avail; Paul forcibly raped her and beat her if she refused.

"It's not rape if we're married. You owe it to me as my wife. So get used to it, Doll"

It had been nine years since that first physical attack, and tonight had been the worst. She had thought discreetly removing her shoes wouldn't cause a big problem, and even after Paul had told her to put them back on, she had not imagined the severe repercussions she would later face. She had thought wrong. As soon as the last guest left, Paul started.

"What the hell do you think you're wearing? You think that slutty dress makes you look nice? You're my wife, not some damn whore! You're gonna pay for flaunting your body around and flirting. I saw you touch Jeremy's arm and laugh at his jokes!!! And then Bill and Mark, and even Megan. Think if you cheat that'll get rid of me?! Well, guess what?! It won't. You're mine! All mine!" he screamed at her as she cowered in the corner.

She tried to say something, anything to reassure him, but there was nothing that would calm him. Tonight was the first time she had even met Megan and had only exchanged a brief hug with her as she left. She had no idea Paul had noticed the sympathetic look Megan had sent Jasmine's way at dinner. Paul would never admit to seeing it because he it had made him feel threatened, which made him feel weak.

To his colleagues, Paul seemed strong, powerful, and in control. In reality, he was incredibly insecure. His insecurity transferred into his marriage. Jasmine was his little wife, his prized possession, and he couldn't lose her no matter what. He liked to think of her as his doll to keep, show off, and control as he deemed desirable. He would remind Jasmine of the fact that she would still be a starving actress and worthless bartender had he not married her, and this kept her right where he wanted her. Also, by moving Jasmine from New York to California, Paul had succeeded in isolating Jasmine from all those who loved her.

While Jasmine was thinking about all of this, Paul was enjoying himself with Amber and the other dancers. He wasn't even worried about his wife. He knew she was questioning why their marriage had gone this way and where it had all gone wrong. He knew what had happened. He had never loved her – only wanted a doll to play with, control, and show off. She had been the one to fall in love, and that had been her weakness and what gave him complete, unbridled control of her.

Jasmine knew she was trapped in a neverending nightmare; she prayed someone, anyone, would reach out to her. Then she remembered the sympathetic look Megan had given her earlier that night. She cried even more. She knew, even with Megan's help, she'd never get away from Paul.

While Jasmine cried herself to sleep and Paul received various sexual favors from Amber at the club, Megan worried about Jasmine. She had failed to reach any conclusions on how to talk to Jasmine alone and offer her help. Jasmine was always with Paul or unavailable. Having watched her own mother go through abuse, Megan knew that was the way Paul had wanted it. The two women would have to find some way to get together without Paul's knowledge. It would be difficult, but essential to Jasmine's survival.

Advice
By E. K. Keith

When a man tells you
"You are beautiful"
Don't believe him
so much
his eyes
are your only mirror

First
his eyes lie
about the perfect clarity
of your skin
in the morning
the smooth curve
of your lip, the dip
of your navel
the hollow
between your breasts
where the memory of a kiss
still lingers

Then
when he hurts you
his eyes lie
about the scars
and blackheads
on your face
your fat, pimpled ass
your big belly
your droopy, lopsided boobs

After he hurts you
you will stand alone
in the bathroom
brushing your teeth
The toothpaste-speckled mirror
will crack
in your eyes

Don't lose your beauty
in a man's eyes

Keep it for yourself

Not for All the Tea in China
By Deborah R. Majors

The hurt is too much to bear,
I fall beneath its weight and skin
my knee. But the trickle
is not noticed by him, only
the inconvenience of helping
me up from the gravel path.

Sitting on the edge
of the bathtub, I tend my wound
alone because he hates the sight
of blood. So do I,
but for a different reason—
it's mine.

I wipe the sand and tweeze
out the tiniest of stones, then dab
more blood and add the salve
before tearing open a Band-Aid.
Holding the wrapper to the sky,
I promise that this is the last time.

From the other room the call,
When's dinner?
Looking into the mirror,
I see his face
when he comes home
tomorrow

and I'm not here.

How Do I Explain What Happened
By Kelly Baker

I left my virginity on the shore of Big Sur, running off
at seventeen with the illusion that two things crashing
leave only foam and wet spots to be remembered.

We left Los Angeles and headed Midwest; I
followed behind the pick-up he drove and watched him
throw things out. I remember the fruit flesh splatter
against the pavement hummed-hot by Michelin
tires looked like the sunset in Sedona, when the heat
makes your eyes blur and shake.

I remember the house we bought in
Kansas next door to his grandmother, across
the street from his sister and her little baby named
Hailey. When love went bad the house began to rot.

My mind is like a block—yours is like a river,
irreverent and illogical. *Here is some direction*, he said
with the back of his fist or the stab of his dick
as he told me he loved me and I cried.

When he picked me up by my head and threw
my body against a wall and I did not die
there, I thought blood would find its way to
bloom if I was patient – and as I slept in the space between
the couch and the coffee table, I waited for my eye to drop
petals into the living room carpet sea, like so many peach pits spit
from moving car windows.

Since then—
I have not known what to say. Most of the time when I talk
about what happened, I do not feel like I am saying anything at
all; my mouth moves simply and detached. My words sound tired
and small, like the flit of insect wings
resting on the leaf of a well-cared-for kitchen plant.

What haunts me is that I cannot recall what I ever loved
about him. I only remember how my feet tucked beneath my bottom
as I cried, the way I rolled underneath the table
like an infant turning in the womb.

Forever and Half a Day
By Eliska Hahn

... that's what you always would say
As you got ice for my swollen face, through letters, over phone lines
Collect calls from jail
"I NEED BAIL!"

"But I will love you, Liskee—for forever and half a day... this is ALL
YOUR FAULT anyway!"

However
I can still taste the blood
And feel the jagged edges of my broken teeth
As my tongue darted across them
In fear and disbelief

Maybe I am all the things you say I am – pathetic, stupid, ugly
But what about her?
She's not yet 2... just a baby... so perfect
What did she do
To deserve to live in this Hell
That burns hotter with each passing moment
This Hell that knows no end
This Hell that will last forever and half a day

I ran barefoot down that gravel road
On that cold February night
Only the light of the moon lit my path
Gripping her tight to my chest, I prayed
"God!! Please rescue us!"
My answer came as you grabbed my long hair
Snatching me backward off my feet
I watched her fall in the dirt as if it took hours
With a growl dripped in hate and Bacardi
You swore, "Do that again and I will kill you both."

But I will love you, Liskee, forever and half a day
I will just never let you get away,
Ever.
I haunt you to this very day
Go ahead and sleep with the light on every night
You silly cow
I occupy not your room, but your mind
You can't run from me now

I kept my promise, Liskee
I didn't lie this time, Liskee
Wherever you go, I will be there, Liskee
Forever and half a day.

Please... if you or anyone you know is in any kind of dating or domestic abuse situation, call your local authorities and get out! It will always, always get worse. May God bless you and keep you.

Apples
By Richard Stokes

The little boy has eaten all of his dinner. The three of us sit in silence, plates pushed back. Through the window I can see hot sun beating down onto the back lawn.

The boy asks timidly if Daddy will come and play in the garden. Daddy mulls this question over for a while. Eventually, with the air of one conferring a great honour, he pronounces: "After pudding."

Nodding sagely, the child selects an apple from the fruit bowl.

"As long," his father adds, "as you eat up all of your apple."

The boy assents readily. He loves fruit of all kinds, but apples are his favourite. I cut the one he's picked up into segments and put them on his plate. He can't quite deal with the pips yet.

"Say thank you to Mummy."

"Thank you, Mummy," says the child indistinctly, mouth full. His father puts a hand on the boy's arm and says, in a low chiding voice, "Aren't you going to offer anyone else some of your pudding?"

Confusion. The boy stares blankly from his father to me, then back again.

"Offer the plate to Mummy." Grubby hands hold the plate out. I shake my head, smiling thanks. The apple goes to Daddy, who takes a piece and snaps it up in two bites of his sharp teeth.

I think I can see what's coming, but I don't know if I can do anything about it. I might be wrong anyway. I hope I am wrong.

The boy eats quickly. He finishes his pudding and immediately makes for the door. At the last minute he stops, remembering, and turns back expectantly.

"Will you play with me now, Daddy?"

There is a pause. The boy's father replies. I see his mouth in slow motion as it frames the word no. I think of trees creaking before they fall, lorries jack-knifing on slippery roads. It is as though I am watching a sad film I have seen many times before, but which never fails to affect me.

"No," he repeats, and waits for the response.

"Why?"

"You didn't eat all of your apple."

The boy runs to the table. He has to get back up onto his chair to check properly. The plate, of course, is empty. He looks up as if to say: more information required.

Daddy's lips curve in a dead-eyed smile.

"You didn't eat the whole apple, did you? I ate some. So I can't play with you."

The tears come now, lots of them, accompanied by an anguished howl of disappointment. Daddy winces at the sudden noise and takes the boy by both arms. The boy wriggles. There will be bruises. He will have to wear a long-sleeved shirt to nursery tomorrow, no matter how hot it is. Daddy holds him and says, "Calm down! Do you understand?"

I always want to say stop it. I want to say he is only little. The boy suddenly cries out in horror. A dark stain appears on the front of his shorts and begins to spread. I smell fresh urine.

"That's filthy. Filthy! Go to your room and wait for me there."

I don't speak. I look down at the empty plate, the knife, the chopping board. I hear the door open and close. Footsteps go up the stairs. The crying recedes.

"He's got to learn." The boy's father grabs another apple from the fruit bowl and bites down on it.

I get up.

The knife comes with me.

I stab it into his left eye, using my free hand to hold the apple in his mouth. He struggles and tries to scream, but the sound has to come out of his nose, making a sort of strangulated equine noise. It isn't very loud. The knife encounters some resistance. I put some more weight behind it. I know that this man is stronger than me, and for a moment I wonder: why doesn't he hit me, push me off? His arms are flapping all over the place but in a random, uncoordinated sort of way. Then I hear a gristly, dropped-eggshell crunch. The blade goes in another couple of inches. The struggling stops.

I leave him sitting there with the apple still in his mouth. I go up to the boy's room, taking care to shut the dining room door behind me.

My son is sitting on his bed. He looks so small. I clean his face and help him change into some dry clothes, by which time he has stopped crying. He holds my hand and says, "Will you play with me now?"

"Yes," I say.

We go down the stairs, past the dining room, through the kitchen door, and out into the garden. Picking up a plastic spade, he says, "Shall we dig to Australia?"

"That's a long way," I say. "We'll have to dig a very deep hole."

Daddy's Girl: A Death
By Deborah R. Majors

The stray had her fill of our chickens
and their eggs
four nights in a row.

Porch lights and gun
blasts were once enough
to force her to make a run for wild woods,

but blood lust drove her hard
to tempt the light of day
and a country girl's rite of passage.

Daddy made me kill the bitch in broad daylight
with his sawed off shotgun,
while headless hens

still jerked
on the red-soaked
feathered ground.

Her dirty brown and white bloodied body
twitched in unison with her prey;
her left eye remembered me.

I cried. And I cried.

My part in death's quaking and shaking
made me shed tears,
made me wail in pain,

Not his leather belt
behind the barn,
welting bare legs

for being Daddy's big sissy-girl.

Only the Moon Knows
By Thelma T. Reyna

...my secrets
incorrigible peeping tom
  cold-eyed
    like him

I smoothe my daughter's Cinderella
sheets beribboned birds twirling 'round
  the golden head   sunshine
doesn't know
  another
    charade   tonight

I'll lie wood beneath his
whiskey breath

My gut is oatmeal
when he
  cold-eyed like the moon
takes our daughter from her bed
he thinks
  I sleep
how can I?
  She mews for
    just a moment then

he slides heavy into me

  I smell her blood

Envy
By E. K. Keith

How I envy
those women
who are raped
by strangers

People
click their tongues
about tight sweaters and short skirts
She's wrong for being
at the wrong place
at the wrong time

When a man
rapes his wife
people just can't believe a woman
would say a thing like that
about her husband,
can you?

Hair
By Eliska Hahn

I guess there are more important things to reflect upon as we enter the last hours of 2011. I'm sure every blogger worth his or her salt will be composing and crafting great reflective blogs about the past twelve months and what they have learned and how they've grown... perhaps citing accomplishments or regrets or life-changing moments... births or deaths... loss and gain. That's pretty typical, but if there is one thing I'm not, it's typical.

My reflection on 2011 is represented by my **Hair**. My **Hair** has always been a source of great controversy since as far back as I can remember. When I was very, very little, my Gran would stack phone books and Sears and Roebuck catalogues on top of a dining room chair and then lift me and balance me on top of the pile so I would be high enough for her to roll my stick-straight **Hair** onto little Lilt perm rollers. My job was to sit very still and hand her the papers she used to gather the ends of my **Hair** so they could be more easily captured and reigned in and twisted around each colorful perm rod. After all of my **Hair** was rolled, Grandma would give me a towel to cover my face and eyes and cautioned me to hold it tight against my forehead as she wet my entire head with the strong-smelling perm solution. Then, we waited. Waiting isn't easy when you're two or three years old. Come to think of it, I'm 40+ years past toddlerhood and I don't think I've found waiting to be any easier at all, but I digress....

I don't recall how many of these home perms I had growing up, but it was definitely in the double digits. Keep in mind, there was nothing wrong with my **Hair** as a child. It was a natural honey-blonde color that took on a beautiful sun-kissed look every summer from playing outside all day and swimming whenever I got the chance. However, my Gran (who also had naturally straight **hair** that she permed regularly) loved curls. God didn't give them to me, so she did.

As I grew older, my **Hair** took on a staring role in my life. I grew up in the 70's and 80's and **Hair** – big bouncy Farrah Fawcett **Hair** that took one hour, two sets of hot rollers, and 1/3 can of Aqua Net (Extra Hold, of course) – was the desired norm. I continued the perming process well past my high school years. I was a young bride, and my husband loved my **Hair** – as long as I kept it the exact same style as when he first met me a few weeks after my 16th birthday. He got very upset if I suggested cutting it or changing the style much. It wasn't really my **Hair**, it was his **Hair** now. I was just responsible for maintaining it.

As you might guess, that marriage didn't last long and you'll be happy to know that I was re-awarded custody of my own **Hair** in the divorce. I have to admit, I went a little crazy with my newly acquired **Hair** freedom. I teased and fluffed and straightened and even colored it (gasp!) for the first time. This was around 1988 and I am proud to say I have not seen my natural **Hair** color since then, save for a few roots. Can I get an Amen?

Another huge turning point in my **Hair** history came in 1998. That was the year my long, beautiful **Hair** was used as a weapon against me by my then-fiance-turned-abuser as he pulled my **Hair** by the handfuls and dragged me down a dirt road in Oregon by it. Several hours (and many beatings) later when the police finally arrested him for assaulting and kidnapping me and my baby, he tried to lie and said, "I didn't touch her!" But my **Hair**, of which much was wound tightly around the buttons on the cuffs of his shirt, told a different story. Within a few weeks of that night, after most of the bruises faded, I drove to the next town over and I demanded that my long, flowing **Hair** be removed. I had it cut up to my ears. No one would drag me by my **Hair** again. Ever. Problem solved.

Well, the loss of my **Hair** didn't solve anything. It just served as a constant reminder of how I let someone continue to control me for years even when there was no **Hair** to pull. I kept my **Hair** fairly short for most of the next 10 years. I was cautious to never let it grow much below my shoulders and rationalized that it was easier to take care of and that, after all, wasn't I getting too old to have long, flowing tresses? Wasn't long **Hair** that could be worn in a pony tail something of youth? Shouldn't I present a more "mature" appearance?

In 2008, I became very ill. I was bedridden for months and months. The only time I was not in bed was when I was at a doctor's appointment or in the hospital. This went on for over a year and a half. I was often too sick to even wash my **Hair**, let alone have the strength to comb it. I remember having to use both hands to steady the comb when I tried. I hardly went to a salon at all those 18 months. I was just too sick. My **Hair** just grew and grew as I laid in bed day after day, week after week, and so on. When I was placed on an experimental medication for my illness in June of 2010, I started to be able to get my life back, but now – for the first time in over 10 years – I had this long **Hair** to contend with. What was I going to do with all of this **Hair**?

I kept the **Hair**. It has been growing like a weed since I made that decision in the summer of 2010. Now it is even longer than it was that night in 1998 when it was used to hurt me and my baby girl. A few months ago on my 45th birthday, I went to my dear friend who is a talented and amazing **Hair** artist and colorist, and he dyed my **Hair** the most bright, beautiful shade of red I had ever seen in my life! When I stood up after he rinsed the color out and saw my reflection for the first time I said, "Would you look at ME!"

My **Hair** and I have come a long way together. I baby it, braid it, curl it, condition it... but most of all, I LOVE IT. It is my **Hair**. My **Hair** is finally mine and, in the words of Lady GaGa, I am my **Hair**.

This year, may you resolve to love and be loved for exactly who you are.

Lovingly dedicated to my first hair stylist: my Grandma, Mary Louise Eye; and my current hair stylist, Rick Stache. I, and my hair, love both of you, always.

My Mahogany Muse
By Bob McNeil

My Mahogany Muse,
    Certain males
    Try to malign and confine
    Your Sojourner Truth mind.
    However, you,
    Sun-hot with fire,
    Burn your way free.

My Mahogany Muse,
    Once hellish hands
    Exert their fervor to hurt,
    You become water
    And swan away.

My Mahogany Muse,
    Soon as injustice
    Attempts to choke us,
    You become air
    That resuscitates with care.

My Mahogany Muse,
    You are Scripture on Sundays,
    Giving the sum
    From wealth-filled wisdom.
    You are my Guidepost to Utopia,
    Providing angel-glazed rays.

My Mahogany Muse,
    You prevent my descent
    Each time I near
    The Foolishness Abyss.
    Blessedness is the bridge
        You built for us to cross.

In the Cold Light of Day
By Deborah R. Majors

In the cold light of day, the wind kicked me
in the stomach and hoisted the truth far
above my reach. The gale whirled Judas Tree
thoughts toward the sea and played air-guitar
lyrics on one knee. It was in the cold
light of day that the sun pinched both cheeks to
force awareness of living more lies. Bold
rays chapped raw red, scolding life's horseshoe
luck and that cold light of day made faults quite
bare stripped down, down to its thongless flesh. Tears
that once glistened with forgiveness now fight
back. I refuse to call them wasted years,
but a challenge that has chiseled me rock
hard, squared for cold light of day's aftershock.

Unknown War
By: Maria Edmonds

There is a war going on inside my head

I reach my trembling hand for solace

Save me!

Save me from the landmines

I am tired of bobbin' and weavin'
Skipping over what I think is that mine
Only to come down on the explosion

In my face

I scream in agony

Not heard

My heart trembles in horror
The horror projected in the front of my mind
Alone I stand wounded
Alone
One thousand people around

And

Ten thousand landmines to skip and avoid
Nobody knows my war waged for minutes, days, months, years

I will never surrender

Dark Skies
By Brenda L. Turner

It was here, in this place that Marianne called home, that the unthinkable had happened. Her father, whom she had always loved but feared, had begun the storm to which his family would be subjected for years to come. Tonight her father had pushed her mother to the floor – her dear mother, who stayed home and only worked at night to take care of her children, who had taught her to read, write, draw, and color, who had the prettiest smile and most loving arms – and physically attacked her in front of her children before sending them to their bedrooms so he could finish his assault. And now, in the middle of the night, Marianne stood here in the foyer of the living room, where it had happened.

Recalling the events of the night, Marianne couldn't remember what that awful fight had been over – something small, probably. It was always something small. Her father didn't like some dishes her uncle had given her mother one night, and as a result of her mother's refusal to give them back, he threw the dishes on the floor, breaking them. Her mother had to clean up the mess. She had loved them because of the geese design; they had matched her geese-themed kitchen. However, because Marianne's father thought they were ugly, his wife was not allowed to keep them.

The fight she tried so hard to remember why it had happened would change her life more than she knew or could even imagine. From that night forward, Marianne's world would be turned upside down, her home converted into a prison from which she would not escape.

Her formerly happy childhood transformed into a nightmare of violence. Constantly afraid, Marianne and her sister, Amber, even made up a game of hiding from the monster. It was a game that made them feel safe; they were able to hide from the imaginary monster who looked like a man when he walked through the door but then changed into a hideous monster when he got mad, which was often – as was the point of their game. Now that she thought about it, the game was more of a sort of practice for when their dad might unpredictably become the monster. It was a game of searching for hiding places and staying hidden until the world was safe again. Oh, how she wished the game had worked. It never did; they could never hide well enough.

The little girl grew more frightened and hopeless as the nightmare continued. One afternoon while one of her friends was over, her dad came home unexpectedly and the fun playtime turned into a game of hiding underneath a blanket inside of Maryanne's bedroom closet, daydreaming and whispering about Maryanne and her family leaving her dad and moving into her friend's house.

The years dragged by as the violence, fear, and depression increased in both duration and magnitude.

As the violence and fear built up, Marianne's fear of her father spun itself into a web of hopelessness, helplessness, depression, and guilt, eventually leading her into a depression so deep she thought she'd never return. Suicidal thoughts overwhelmed her until she could see no other way out. Holding the sleeping pills in her hand, Marianne sat on the floor of her bedroom thinking about the past, the present, the future, searching for a reason to live.

Flashbacks came in waves, haunting her; violent nightmares of her father's cruelty flooding her thoughts. Moments of terror – the night she woke up to her mother screaming because Marianne's father was strangling her, her mother being beaten with a belt because she had dared to defend her daughters against unfair punishment, the afternoon her father bruised her mother's ribs despite Marianne and her sister's attempts at protecting her, her mother's cries as she was raped by Marianne's father, the bruise she saw on her mother's leg that covered most of her outer thigh from being kicked. It went on and on.

Then there was the abuse Marianne and her sisters had suffered at the hands of a man who was supposed to love and protect them. Marianne had been beaten so many times she had lost count. One particular Thanksgiving a couple years before, Marianne had been strangled by her father. This memory brought back all the anger and bitterness Marianne felt toward the legal system and her mother for failing her.

She had gone with her mother to the Assistant State Attorney's office to speak with the detectives and the prosecutor assigned to the case. Marianne lied to protect her mother and her mother lied to keep her children in the home. Her mother had lied from the very beginning when the Department of Children and Families first began an investigation when Marianne was only six years old. The investigation was ongoing for three years with Marianne's parents taking court ordered parenting classes, attending counseling, and the ever-present fear of the children being placed in foster care. This was when Marianne had learned to fear social workers and lie about her home life.

Marianne had wanted to seek help, to tell the truth, but was too scared of being taken away from her mother. She had hoped and wished she could be taken away from her father, but due to wanting to stay with her mother and sisters, she lied. The family secret was safe as long as fear was ingrained in Marianne and the system continued to prove time and again that it would fail to help Marianne's mother. Help, as defined by Marianne, was forcing her father to leave and helping her mother establish her own independence.

By Marianne's standards, everyone, even God – yes, God – had failed her. Then the question came that if God failed her, why would she want to be with Him in heaven? God, she reasoned, was the only one who could explain the enormous suffering she had endured. God was also a being of unending love and goodness, and Heaven was an indescribable paradise where pain, darkness, and fear were nonexistent. Heaven was where Marianne longed to be – away from her father and in the arms of her Heavenly Father who loved her unconditionally.

All these thoughts brought Marianne back to the question at hand – whether or not she should take her own life in exchange for an eternity of peace. She had suffered so long, and still not seeing any hope, she decided to end her suffering the only way she could imagine. The pills promised an escape out of her nightmare.

The moment had come... but just as her hand holding the pills reached her mouth, a voice in her head whispered, "You know we care about you, don't you?" It was the voice of her youth minister who had said that exact phrase out of the blue when she had been talking with him over the phone just two days before.

With tears streaming down her face, she went into the bathroom, flushed the pills down the toilet, sat down, and cried. There was someone who cared; there was still love in the world. A beam of wonderful hope shone through the dark skies of her life like a ray of sunshine through unending storm clouds.

Real Women Bare Scars
Eleanor Leonne Bennett

Again it Happens
By D. Smith

blood flowing down her face,
mingling with her tears and falling
from her chin.

doorknobs are hazardous...
clumsy bitch fell again.

try to be more careful.

dinner was late, cold, or needed salt;
any excuse will do—
cold beer fuels hot temper.

how many times this year
pack your shit and go
but to where, I'm all you got.

pleading makes it worse
eye swollen shut
your scars are filled with my love.

til death do us part;
only way you'll leave
with one of us lying cold.

The Cold
By Michael K. Moore

It's cold today.
It's cold every day.
It's just another thing Dad uses to argue with Mom about.
They only argue when it gets this cold.
Dad drinks a little more.
Mom cries a little more.
Dad swings his fists a little more.
Mom's face bruises a little more.
I'm scared a little more.
I hug my teddy a little more.
Sometimes I'd rather be outside.
It's too cold in here.

Snap
By Thelma T. Reyna

It had to be a snap decision: to help him or let him die.

With no one watching, no one knowing.

Not even Sal, delirious as he was with pain. As blind as he was with eyelids red and swollen shut, blood filling his nostrils, coagulations caking his face and jamming his throat, purplish blobs spat out rhythmically on the dirt, on his shirt, on his brother's hands holding his lapels in balled fists. Sal wouldn't know the difference.

His brother's fists had broken Sal's cheekbone moments earlier, just after Sal fired the gun at him and missed, just after Sal sliced their mother and set fire to the house. He'd been a wild man so long now, nothing surprised. Little brother gone wild, witnessed by decades of tirades and tears, by father now dead, by mother bleeding on the kitchen mat, moaning for the two sons she lost so long ago and she'd lose for good tonight. Two sons. Two brothers tethered tightly in childhoods gone awry.

Sal and Mike. Mike and Sal. They'd been interchangeable in times long gone.

They had stood together against their father since the beginning. What is it that makes a father turn monster? What lets a father's hands throttle, burn, cut, and choke a child's hope? What enables a mother to watch and weep and sweep her children in the dustbin every morning? Sal didn't know. Mike didn't know, but their little children hearts knew that standing together against the monster was the only white knight on their horizon.

And the years passed nonchalantly, like they do for such children, just rolling over and over like smoke from fires in forests too deep to measure. Rolling over and over into bloody noses and broken teeth, into tales at school that enabled two sons to make it through another day, teachers blind as mothers blind, teachers tricked as neighbors tricked, and the years just rolled over one another, over and over, and over and over.

Until Sal grew big. Bigger than his father, his hands heavier than his, his tongue swollen with venom that silenced his father's mouth. Sal's boots were swifter than the monster's, till, month after month, year over year, the monster broke and whitened and had tissue-paper hands that lay limp on sofa arms, and Sal ruled the roost. Jack

Daniels was Sal's friend, his companion till the monster's end, for even monsters die when their poison sticks in veins and clogs the flow of terror. So the monster died near midnight, head and back bones broken, mother blind as mothers are, and one son so far, far away from monster dyings and son slayings.

Mike had stood by Sal, and came to town to put the monster in the ground. But he saw their father had re-birthed in Sal. The child is father of the man, some say, but the father is child, too. And Mike the survivor, the first son, the one who had some rank in the beginnings, buried the monster and feared its spawn.

That night, Sal drowned his vestiges of humanity in Jack Danny. Their aproned mother, mouth pressed cold, swept trails of debris into familiar corners. The sight of Mike—first-born man, hands calm, looking unwounded in the world but wounded at the monster's death as he gathered up the old man's things and stuffed them into alley bins—was too much for Sal to bear. He snapped, and Hell had never spat a greater fury.

What is it that pits brother against brother, flesh against blood, blood against flesh? What is it that wipes pain against pain until obliteration makes pain come back again? A dessicated soul can do little more than snap, a twig broken in two, two broken halves, two broken sons, never one again.

When Sal snapped and cut his mother's breast and shot their father's pistol at Mike's head, and threw the match onto the cushions of the sofa where his old man snapped in two and died, Mike snapped, too. The brothers' legs and arms twisted together as they tumbled onto the porch and rolled onto the dirt. Mike's fists pummeled his kid brother's face, breaking nose and teeth, like the monster. To kill a monster, Mike became the monster. The child is the father, and the father is the child, and the cycle plays itself unending.

Two parts of a broken twig, each half breaking into more than two. Mike stood and tried to find his balance. He made his choice. He staggered in the house to save his mother. The rivulets of blood flowed from Sal's mouth, his eyes, his ears, staining earth in a greatly expanding circle that circumscribed Sal's body faintly, flames shaking in the fire that consumes all monsters.

Summer Heat

By Melissa Salazar

His rage
Caused hurt
Black, blue… blood.
And fear;
The kind that remains nameless
But has a face.
Summer is when
I learned that hatred
Could be felt like August heat.
Red temper
Left marks on soft skin.
My mother's body branded
By the hands of the one she loved most.
She never left….
She endured many scorching summers.

Secrets
Karen Jones

Anyone Who Asks the Part
By Enigma

There is no
sense

In what
she does...

No meaningful
direction

To her
lust...

Blindly blowing
kisses

In the
dark...

She will take
anyone

Who asks
the part...

The faulted
actions

Of her
dealings

By her
unknown

In real
feelings...

You see...

To her so-
called

Husband

An object

His to
own

There was no
sense

Her senseless
acts

Because her
husband

Broke her
back...

She only
wanted

To be
seen

Did not
intend

To be
unclean...

She thought
the takers

Of the
part

Somehow
could see

Her broken
heart...

And what
she did

Tore me
apart...

What happens
when

A love is
sought

But never
given

Leading to
these

Bad
decisions

So that
all she
got

Were the
takers

Of the
part

Who did
not

Really

See her
Heart...

Forbidden Fruit
By Katie Rendon Kahn

Strawberry blond
Apple of Daddy's eye
Nectar stolen
Peach bruised
Cherry popped

Honeydew skin, plowed
And planted
With sour grapes
And thorny
Blackberry vines

To bear more fruit
To be groped,
Peeled and squeezed.
Picked long before
Ripe.

Mercy in the Middle
By Eliska Hahn

It was the summer of 1976... I was getting ready to turn 10 years old that September. My family and I lived in a townhouse/apartment complex in the small town in rural West Virginia where I was born. I was a tomboy, all pigtails and dirt, and loved spending dawn to dusk playing outside every day and trying to master the skateboard I got the previous Christmas from Santa. There was a nice, friendly, elderly man who lived in one of the bottom apartments next to our town home who would always wave and say, "Hello," as he carried his groceries in from his car.

I can still see that car. It was a four-door olive green sedan. One day after he had been to the grocery store, he was sitting on his front porch, called me over, and presented a big bag of Brachs candy which was sold in bulk at our local grocery. He asked me if I would like some, and I of course eagerly said, "Yes!" As I was exploring all the goodies in the white bag with its trademark pink and purple stripes around the center, something so strange happened. This man reached down the front of my tank top and began rubbing my chest.

Now I was brought up not to question my elders and I just remember feeling afraid, so I grabbed a few pieces of candy and said, "thank you," over my shoulder as I ran back toward my house.

As time went by, he became more and more insistent that I come visit him on his porch or in his car and he would always give me candy and rub my private parts and attempted to expose himself to me. At 9 1/2 I didn't know I was being molested. I didn't even know what that meant, but even at that young age I instinctively knew that something was very, very wrong and found it upsetting on the deepest of levels.

I can't remember if he told me not to tell anyone, but I was too ashamed to. I wish I could tell you why I went back each time he called me over, but I don't really know for sure. I think I was afraid not to go because he might tell my parents something bad about me and I would get into trouble. He began to pressure me and he was old enough to be my grandfather and I tried to respect his wishes for a visit and hope and pray the next time would be different and he wouldn't touch me. My prayers went unanswered.

Later that summer, he died. I remember seeing the ambulance in the parking lot and watching them wheel his body out, covered with a white sheet. Everyone in the neighborhood was gathered around talking about what a tragedy it was that he died alone. I had such mixed emotions. Part of me was thankful he was gone and I wouldn't have to endure the shame and anxiety of what I was feeling or any more visits. I was happy, angry, confused, relieved, and sad all at the same time. I thought you were always supposed to just feel really sad when someone died, weren't you?

Child molestation is rampant in this country. Current statistics state that one out of every four girls will be sexually molested by the time they graduate high school... and one out of every six boys. I was one of the "lucky" ones because it didn't last long... just that summer in '76, but some young girls endure this for years, every day, every night. Let's face it, ONCE is too many times and can leave life-long damage.

In 1991 I heard a song by Amy Grant about childhood sexual abuse called Ask Me. I have listened to this song hundreds if not thousands of times and it helped so much to heal what was so broken inside of me for so long.

Thanks for this song, Amy. Now I have found a peace that has only come from God. He has made me feel whole again and has healed these wounds over time with His grace and unconditional love. I still sleep with a night light in the hall but He is working on me. I have been renewed by the blood of Christ. "Because of the Lord's great love we are not consumed, for His compassions never fail. They are new every morning; great is your faithfulness." (Lamentations 3:22-23) No matter what has happened, the Word promises, "For I am convinced that neither death nor life, neither angels nor demons, neither the present or the future, nor any powers, neither height or depth, nor anything else in all creation, will be able to separate us from the love of God that is Christ Jesus our Lord." (Romans 8:38)

This is a fallen world filled with every imaginable evil but we are told to take heart, "for everyone born of God overcomes the world...." (1 John 5:4)

If you or anyone you know is a victim of sexual abuse, please don't put off seeking help. The 24-hour hot line is 800-656-HOPE.

Return to Sleeping
By Frances Pauli

I wake from nothing;
No sound, no movement,
Your angelic face
Above me, staring
Lit softly from the light drifting
Through our curtains;
Still, motionless above me,
Your eyes stone.

The second time I've seen them
Empty.

Your hand hovering, raised
To strike me,
Frozen as I watch you
See me.

Then falling softly, weightless
To my cheek,
Tender, caressing.

So intimate, that gentle
Feather to cheek;
So deadly,
The sweetest touch you've ever offered.

You roll away—return to sleeping,
Your back a wall of covers
As I tremble in our bed.

Rather Die Standing
By Diesta Kaiser

I'd rather die standing
Than live on my knees, begging
For your love
For my life
For the pain to end
The tears to stop
The bruises to fade
But once they do
You push me into a corner
And put them back again

But I'll stand up
And fight on my own
Like a cornered animal
With nothing to lose
Because that's what I let you
Turn me into

I found my self-esteem
And now I'm free
With my life ahead of me
The bruises and broken bones
Gone forever
Finally rid of the shadows
And the fear in my eyes

I'm never going back
To black eyes and bloody lips
A selfish master
Beating me to my knees
Telling me I'm not strong enough
Not good enough
To cover his own inadequacies

Because you were just afraid
I would see myself
As I really am
Not the way you wanted me to be
And that I would realize
I was stronger
Than you wanted to admit
And that I could beat you

I turned to him
For support
Afraid he would forsake me
Because I was broken
Dejected
Convinced I deserved
Everything you did

But he looked through the shadows
Walked with me through
The ruins of my mind
My heart, my soul,
My body
That you had left behind
Picked up the pieces
Put them back together

He healed the wounds
You left in the wake
Of your fear and anger
Kissed away the tears
Smoothed away the scars
You put on my heart, soul, mind, body
Showed me who I could be
If I only believed
In myself
In him
In love

He picked me up
Off my knees
Believed in me
When I couldn't
Told me I was enough
That I always would be
Loved me
Throughout it all

Held me
When the memory
Of what you did
Came too close to the surface
When your words
Rang too loudly in my head
When my mind began to crack
When I couldn't live with myself
And I woke in the middle of the night
Crying and screaming in pain and fear

He made me see
How strong I really was
Made me see
That you couldn't
Control me anymore
Because he would extinguish
All you did
With a kiss
A touch
A word

Strength and Beauty
By Katherine Shirley

For years I thought sadness
Was beautiful
Minor keys sang lonely songs
With haunting loveliness
Then I found you
And knew the reason
People still dream
Of laughter

The Truth about Spiritual Abuse

By Victoria M. Reynolds

For most people, the words "spiritual abuse" conjure up images of Catholic priests and their sexual encounters with little boys or ministers who promote child abuse as necessary for breaking a child's will. We have all heard stories of murder in the name of God and nearly every war in our planet's history has been justified, in some form, by religious interpretation. But spiritual abuse is much more than the human rights abuses that are justified by religious opportunists; it is abuse of the human spirit.

Spiritual abuse, similar to emotional abuse, leaves no physical evidence. The only evidence of its existence are the countless lives that are riddled with shame, fear, and lack of fulfillment. Spiritual abuse is the most painful and difficult abuse to diagnose and to heal. Long after we have left our religions behind and received therapy for the mind, the trauma to the soul prevents us from being all that we have the ability to be. The trauma reaches into the very core of who we are. It prevents us from having a truly connecting relationship with ourselves and others, and prevents us from experiencing any real form of spirituality.

Many of us were raised in religions that controlled us through fear-based beliefs and dogmatic practices. The controlling fear of those beliefs is the root of all spiritual abuse and gives rise to opportunists. While free-will-choice is a promise we are all told that God ensures us, many of us live in the ever-present fear of making choices that will damn us for eternity. In that fear we live our lives in constant terror, unable to make conscious choices and using our free will against ourselves and others, not recognizing that we are perpetuating the abuse. These fear-based religious beliefs prevent us from accessing our own spiritual truth. The truth that we are all born worthy, that we are all born in perfection, and that we are all born with the potential for greatness. Our beliefs prevent us from knowing the truth that we are all one with God and the truth that we are always learning, growing, evolving, and expanding. The guilt, shame, and fear that result from our religious beliefs prevent us from recognizing and fulfilling the very reason for our physical existence.

When we are able to realize that the lack of joy and fulfillment in our lives stems from the trauma to our soul, we are then able to begin the work of healing that trauma. All of the work we do to keep our minds and bodies healthy is in vain if the soul is damaged. While spiritual abuse and soul trauma are still relatively new concepts, there are talented spiritual healers who know how to work with this form of abuse and bring healing to it. From the perspective wholeness, we are then able to see our own divine potential and experience truly joy-filled lives, without constant fear of eternal consequences. We are able to recognize that the wounds have been healed when all that we feel is love.

Recognition
By Mari Maxwell

You do not look and see,
gaze upon the bloodied walls within you.
You fear the fist, the bloodied nose.
The carnage.
Because you do, it returns time and time again.
Seeking. Nudging. Burrowing.
Shrieking for solace.
It will not cease until you become brave brothers, sisters.
Grab the demon by the horns.
Dig deep, deep within.
There, rooted and steadfast, is that which helped child endure,
survive.
That took courage, took Herculean strength.

Somewhere buried deep it lies in hope,
Begging for flight. Its right to be.
Love?

Love that which survived.
Parent, nurture that which was torn asunder.
Because if you do, I promise a flower-filled garden.
Laden with friend, fauna, and life.
The past sifted with present, in the clay of your garden, will flourish.
As it should, my siblings.
As it should.

Take that broken child by the hand.
Look it in the eye.
Remind it of its immaturity, its vulnerability.
Let it grieve as adult that which it hasn't.
Lost child.
Broken child.
Battered child.

Let the two merge –
Strength with strength –
To fully live the life you were meant to.

I had no choice in my journey – maybe you, too.
I have not wanted these paths fraught with hate, toxins,
and venom.
Neither have I sought a cause or mission.
I just cannot bear the suffering, the battered shells of life
that deserve to bloom.
Their perfumes soothe and calm the deep dark waters.

You huddle childlike, clutching shame that isn't yours.
Take my hand.
Let child and adult reunite.
I won't let go.

Hand...
Nor path.

Mother Portraits
Eleanor Leonne Bennett

The Battle of Voices
By Logan Fisher

The underwear on the floor of the foyer was a warning. The shredded crotch mocked my naivety and sucked away the celebratory bliss that I was feeling.

All day, the voice of Triumph had exclaimed one word: "FREE!" Free from sweaty palms and a nervous stomach. Free from horrific bellowing and name calling. Free from feelings of inferiority. Free. I had revolted and won. I was liberated from Steve, the tyrant, the dictator. I was free from my hateful husband.

While Steve packed his things at the home that we would no longer share, I spent my "Independence Day" at the beach where the freedom-feeling mixed with sand, soggy sandwiches, my sons, and most remarkably, smiles on all three of us.

George, my youngest, squealed with delight as he dipped his toddler toes in the water on the shoreline. My oldest, Adam, usually timid and pensive, mustered up bravery to dive over the buoy line into the dangerous deep end. I gazed upon them with a giddiness that I couldn't reign in. Triumph washed over me in waves, soothing and cooling hot spots and smoothing over holes dug with sharp shovels. It shouted, "This is how life will ALWAYS be from now on!" Driving for the first time toward a home that was absent of Steve, my wistful heart couldn't help but dream of more moments like today.

Now, in the foyer and still excited by the events of the day, a naked and sandy-bottomed Adam danced around me. Oblivious to the underwear, he squealed, "I have to go potty! I have to go potty!" His bare feet took him quickly down the hall. With a cloudy mind, I bent down to get a closer look at the underwear. Our orange-handled scissors lay next to them. Apprehension kept me from picking up either item. I was still unsure of why they were there. More importantly, why were the underwear cut? Fear, that familiar beaten voice, one that had been rigorously trained by years of emotional abuse, urged me to see the truth. Edges of cold panic began to seep into my bones, but still beaming from the day, I wouldn't permit it to creep further.

I told myself, the independent me, that I no longer had to live with the voice of Fear. In fact, I would use a different voice to command it to halt. Albeit a whisper, a new voice, Independence, decided that there must be a logical solution to the underwear that was now clenched in my right hand. Looking at them closely, my thoughts groped and my eyes scanned the room. The answer lay on the couch: a sword – more importantly, Captain Hook's sword.

Adam had been going through a pirate phase. At any time during the day, you could find him fighting an imaginary Peter Pan, screaming, "Arrghh get back, ye land lubbers!" Perhaps he cut them up to wear as a sort of headpiece. A slight smile broke out on my lips. What a photo that would have made! My lungs filled with a deeply relieved breath. The voice of Independence congratulated me for my calm approach to solving the mystery.

"Mommy, I'm bleeding! There's blood!" My satisfaction was short-lived as a howl pierced the silence. Adam was shrieking in the bathroom.

Dropping the underwear, I fled and found my four-year-old standing in the middle of a surreal scene. The bathroom floor (THE BATHROOM?!) was full of broken dishes. The shards lay like puzzle pieces, some right side up, others upside down in ceramic disarray. I immediately recognized the fruit pattern from my wedding china. Stunned and frightened, Independence let go of logic and retreated to a dark corner. Fear, my old friend, saw its chance and took over. It commanded that familiar hot rushing anxiety to begin a full-fledged march from the edges of my consciousness to the parts of my mind that housed reality.

Adam was hopping from foot to foot. A droplet of his blood smeared on one of the bigger pieces of shattered plates.

"Adam!" I said as firmly as I could. "You need to stop hopping and stand still or you will cut yourself again!" I tiptoed cautiously through the dangerous maze, scooped him up, and carried him out.

Setting Adam down on the kitchen counter, I cooed and soothed him. The cut was superficial, a jagged centimeter, shaped like the letter J. My shaky hands wiped it carefully and repaired it with a band-aid. I announced, "All better!" He smiled a relieved smile and I kissed his forehead.

"Pirates!" Spotting an imaginary foe, Adam bounded off the counter to begin a new adventure. I envied the ease with which his troubles went away. If only a kiss could fix the madness in the house.

I decided that nap time was best so the glass could be picked up. Adam flopped down onto his mattress. I sat next to him and absent-mindedly stroked his soft cheek. Wrapping his arms around my neck, he pulled my ear to his mouth.

"I didn't break the glass, Mommy. I am sorry. I didn't break the glass."

"Of course you didn't, sweetie!" I smoothed his golden hair and covered his face with kisses. "Don't you worry about it. By the time you wake up, I will have picked up that mess!"

Shutting his bedroom door, new voices, Rage and Terror, combined with familiar Fear. Each voice shouted, trying to be heard, fighting for control of my mind's microphone. My head throbbed with the mixture. Collapsing onto the couch, I crossed my arms in front of me and held tight to keep from shaking. Thankfully Adam's cut was small. But I was keenly aware of what could have happened to my sweet child. I shuddered at the thought of it. Independence may have been able to explain away the shredded underwear, but the smashed china AND the underwear... there was only one explanation for that.

I knew. Of course I knew. After 10 years, it was an inevitability. Every muscle, bone, and every type of voice housed in my crowded consciousness shouted to me the culprit. My husband, Steve, had sent a message. He didn't physically reign over me anymore, but mentally, he'd hold on strong. Steve's destruction was meant to keep Fear alive and in charge. As long as it remained, I wouldn't make it on my own... just as he had always said. He needed me to keep being that scared woman. He would do anything to keep control. That meant he wouldn't stop at just underwear and china. No, knowing him the way that I did, I knew he had set more traps before his departure. For a moment, I wanted to curl up in a ball and hide, but even after years of abuse, a scant amount of the voice Strength remained. It ordered me to stand straight and tall and face what I needed to face head on.

With a heavy heart and the joy felt earlier in the day seemingly miles away, I set out to search for more destruction. Opening the back door, I descended the two steps to the garage. Knocked back by the sight before me, I clung to the doorway so that my legs wouldn't give way. True to his evil form, my husband had continued his Kong-like rampage. Cupboards hung from bent hinges. Rakes, bikes, and shovels lay in a tangled pile, and glass littered the floor. This time the shards came from the windows on the door to the backyard.

Panic came with large teeth that bit into me. Its sharp gnashes were too much for me to bear. I sank to the steps of the garage. Independence now felt more like solitary confinement. I needed help.

I couldn't do this. I couldn't face this alone. Who could I call? Like most women battered by their husbands, Steve had methodically isolated me from friends and loved ones. I literally didn't have one solid relationship I could call upon for assistance. Once again, Strength mustered up enough vim to whisper a solution. Shocked at what the voice suggested, but too exhausted to argue, I called my parents.

A week earlier, I sat in my mother and father's kitchen like a chastized child, head down, tears plopping on the table in dramatic drops and a napkin twisting in my nervous fingers. They doled out their shame heartily hoping perhaps that I would change my mind about this "crazy notion of divorce."

Tomas and Jan were pillars of the community, small-town-dwellers seeping in success, former PTA presidents and heads of the counsel at our local Episcopal church. When I was a little girl, my mother was my Girl Scout and Brownie leader and sent in birthday treats to school that rivaled Martha Stewart. My father, a well-known coach, was a beloved teacher for 30 years and had established a popular running program for children. Despite all of these towny credentials, their proudest, most sensible accomplishment (and the other small-town-dwellers agreed) was that they were the parents of four successful girls who they had raised to be image-conscious and who were aware of avoiding choices that would call for gossip and shame. With their wisdom and guidance, Tom and Jan procured four daughters who were credits to the status of their family, who would never do anything that would cause judgment from the harsh voices of a small community, and therefore never bring humiliation to their parents.

Accordingly, it wasn't surprising or stunning that on that day, a week ago, my parents sat utterly baffled at the disgraceful scuttlebutt surrounding my marriage that had been caught in a gossip wind storm, and much to mom and dad's chagrin, had taken over the community. Their disappointed faces glowered down at me.

"What did we do wrong?" my mother moaned. "Why do you insist on embarrassing this family?" The misery that my decisions inflicted made me wince. Feelings of shame engulfed me. That day, the voice of Guilt told me that I deserved the blows, and so I sat, silently waiting for the inquisition.

The story, first heard through the network of small-town busybodies, was that my husband of five years was moving out. The details were seedy. Steve found out that I was having an affair with a teacher that I worked with every day. I didn't do much to deny it. Flaunted it, really, with the hope – I am ashamed to admit – that it would hurt him as much as he'd hurt me over the years. Unfortunately, what started out as an act of revenge turned into a genuine love, perhaps obsession, and one night during one of our clandestine phone calls, Steve barged into the room, ripped the phone from my hand, and threatened to kill the co-worker. To compound the dishonor, that same co-worker decided to press charges, and our illustrious local newspaper picked up the story only to splash it across the front page. According to the article, Steve would have to stand trial in front of a judge that happened to be the co-worker's distant family member. There was a real chance, at last, that he would have to pay for his violence and cruelty. As the scandal grew larger and larger, feeling the pressure of small town chatter, that colleague took a "midnight train to Georgia," adding fuel to the fire and leaving me to look like the town Jezebel.

My parents saw this turpitude as the ultimate catastrophe. They lamented and scolded and begged and pleaded for me to reconsider and stay together with Steve. Reconciling would make the newspaper article look like it may have gotten the facts incorrect. For Mom and Dad, the humiliating headlines were an end to the years of image-making that they had woven. It was the end of their small-town superiority, and to them, the end of their lives as they once knew it.

I, on the other hand, saw this scandal as an opportunity for freedom, my one chance. Reconciling was not even the smallest notion. I finally had leverage, something with which to bargain. Even though I felt obligated to sit and listen to my tormented parents, I didn't feel bound to honor their requests. It was too late. A deal had already been struck with my abusive husband. I persuaded the co-worker to drop the charges on the condition that Steve would finally move out and leave me and my boys alone.

Make no mistake, my parents did a masterful job of getting the voice of Guilt to float to the top of my jumbled emotions, but Intelligence wouldn't be pushed around, and therefore, my mind could not be changed. Knowing that they faced defeat, Mother and Father used the last weapon in their arsenal.

"We have never been as disappointed in you and your choices as we are at this moment. If you don't get back together with Steve, then you stand alone. We are disgusted!" That is how I left them in the kitchen that day: disappointed, defeated, and disgusted with me.

Now, back in the garage, Mom and Dad arrived minutes after my calling them. They found me sitting on the steps, head in hands and sobbing. Among chokes and sputters, an almost infantile voice blurted out, "Mom, what should I do? Should I call the police?"

As they surveyed the grim garage, another voice, Helplessness, emerged from the crowd of voices. It came from the recesses of my brain where a little child resides. I imagined being scooped up in my mother's arms to be soothed and cooed as I had done with Adam earlier. I reached out to her. She remained where she stood, stiff and haughty. My father's voice sliced through the tension.

"Call the police? Yeah, that's all we need. Why don't we give this town more to talk about by fueling the fire with a police report?"

His stern and cutting response acted like a stinging hand across my cheek, and although not what I needed, snapped me back to reality. What a fool I had been to imagine compassion. After 28 years of rigidity and strict mores from my parents, I could no more expect kindness from them than I could expect a blind man to see.

At the curt suggestion from my mother, we began to look for more damage. With leaden feet, I stepped carefully through the mess, making half-hearted attempts to right some of it. I pushed open the door, emptied of glass, in order to survey our large backyard. Steve's garden (which he took much better care of than the humans in his life) looked as though a bulldozer had destroyed it. Clumps of dirt, mangled marigolds, roots, and vines lay in crooked piles like pick-up sticks. I turned cautiously to the right and the breath caught in my throat. Like something out of the movie "Edward Scissor Hands," the flowering crab tree, George's flowering crab tree planted in honor of his birth, had been cut to the trunk. Most of the branches were stripped of leaves and hung from wood threads like men in gallows.

We spent most of the afternoon in utter silence trimming, raking, sweeping, and cutting. To their credit, my parents worked like mules, their grim faces set and determined. For all that it was worth, the house was cleaner and the yard neater than it had started out being that morning. I feebly made an attempt to thank them for their "kindness and support." As I reached out to hug my mother, her body stiffened and her hands instead grasped my shoulders and pushed my body out to arms length. She stared directly and purposely into my eyes, and I saw in hers determination.

Once again, in the corner of my weary mind, the voice of Child hoped against all hope that she would offer something for me to hold on to. It willed her to tell me that I was not alone and that she'd be there for me no matter the humiliation, no matter the gossip, no matter the torture Steve had planned.

Then, another voice, Cynicism, laughed at Inner Child naivety. The sinister sound of that laugh weakened the Child's resolve, but it could not be deterred. And so, all three of us, Child, Cynic, and I waited for her to speak.

"Daughter," she said. Her voice was flat so that I couldn't read it. Her lips turned up slightly. A smug smile?

"You have made your bed. You will have to lie in it."

Cynic laughed his triumphant laugh. Child wept, and I, stunned, stood silent while my mother feigned a sympathetic look and patted me on the cheek. As I watched my parents get into their car and leave, a cheerful, "Mommy!" brought me back. My boys were awake.

Dinner and bath time, pajamas and book time, tuck-me-in time, and don't-forget-my-drink time helped to pass the evening quickly and provided me with welcome distractions, but now in the emptiness of the house, the anguish flooded back. Eager to keep it at bay and exhausted from the day, I decided to sleep. Fear returned and tried to talk me into sleeping on the couch with the lights on, TV blaring, and a knife within reach, but Strength had not been extinguished completely and his determination to be free of the crippling Fear caused me to head to my bedroom.

Reaching for the doorknob, a distressing realization took hold of me. For all that had happened during the day, Adam's cut, my parents, the clean up, I hadn't had the time to check my bedroom. If Steve would destroy rooms as banal as the bathroom and garage, surely he wouldn't leave such an intimate room like the bedroom damage-free! I faced the possibility that the nightmare may not be completely over.

A debate began to ring out, the battle of the voices. Fear pleaded with me to run back down the hall.

"Open the bedroom door during the light of day!" it screamed.

Independence scoffed at Fear. "Under no circumstance will you cower because of Steve again. Buck it up and open the door!"

Even after all the events of the afternoon, the Child in me still wanted to pick up the phone. "Call your mom!" it cried.

Agreeing with all the voices but knowing that I needed to make a decision if only for the reason of getting it over with, I eventually sided, reluctantly, with Independence.

Gingerly, I pushed open the door, proud that Independence won out but deeply afraid of what I would find there. Groping with shaking hands and fear-prickled skin, I reached for the light and snapped it on. Rivers of ice flowed through my veins and fists of nausea pounded me. This time, it wasn't one pair of underwear that served as a warning, it was all my underwear. A few lay in a pile in the middle of the bed. Some were strewn on the floor. A couple, violently flung, hung from the curtain rods and shelves. All had been shredded in the crotch like the pair in the foyer.

Strength was snuffed out and Child retreated. Fear pushed Independence aside and took over. My knees gave way underneath me. I dropped onto the bed, biting hard onto the back of my hand to alleviate the pain that had lodged in my stomach.

The underwear was a warning. It served as a vision of what was to come. Like the crotches, Steve would shred every fiber of me for finding the strength to leave him. Lying down, I drew my knees to my chest, terrorized by the knowledge that was dawning on me. The tyrant and dictator had declared war, and in a way, my perfidious parents would be his troops.

Independence would not come without a fight.

A Song for Sheroes
By Bob McNeil

Women, make men comprehend,
Women, make men comprehend,
Women,
Make men comprehend
That each sister
Has a Harriet Tubman
Prepared to seek
A place where men
Do not abuse their Queens,
A place that erects Jewels of Respect.

Women, make men comprehend,
Women, make men comprehend,
Women,
Make men comprehend
That each sister
Has a Shirley Chisholm
Prepared to shake and make every state
Understand that liberation
Must not become a membership card
Only given to men.

Women, make men comprehend,
Women, make men comprehend,
Women,
Make men comprehend
That each sister
Has a Dr. Mae C. Jemison
Entering a NASA shuttlecraft
That ascends to a time
Where gender mistreatment ends.

Women, make men comprehend,
Women, make men comprehend,
Women, make men comprehend.

How Anger and Education Saved Me from Suicide
By Henriette Eiby Christensen

Seven years ago, I came out of a 12-year verbally abusive relationship not knowing what had happened.

First relief, then not understanding why I felt so bad, and I kept feeling like the world would be a better place without me in it.

Then ANGER. No way was I going to let him continue to have that kind of power over me – I had to understand everything, not only for myself, but also for my three children. And so I started writing and observing. Along the way I found that I wasn't just writing my own story. It was relevant to so many people it wasn't funny.

My ex-husband is a very smart and handsome man. I was more of a pleaser – eager to accommodate other people's needs. I was willing to toss and turn every single pebble of my body and soul to accommodate him.

There was always an element of truth to every abusive thing he said about me or others, so I was kept in a state of constant confusion and soul searching. He never hit me. He never came home drunk. We shared a bank account.

But he slowly drew life out of me with his words.

I did everything wrong – the way I kept our house wasn't how he liked it. I had too much "stuff." I was too "laid-back." He used "positive" critique to belittle me. He would cover his verbal abuse up with, "I'm only being honest." He would withhold sex, calling me nymphomaniac because he couldn't perform. He would call me names and so much more.

My friends and family slowly evaporated from our life.

Here is the part which is very hard to explain… why I stayed. I understand that this is sometimes difficult to comprehend from the outside looking in. You see, I was a stay-at-home mom in Denmark and very isolated. In Denmark, being a stay-at-home mom is frowned upon. Having a job is much more valued. So I was alone. Alone in my beliefs that my children were much more important than any job could possibly be.

An easy target, you might say. Yes. I no longer had a network. I no longer had an income. I had no self-esteem or self-worth. No special skills which might help me create an income. My education was outdated. And I was stuck. Emotionally and financially stuck.

One day, he decided that we needed a second income, so he pushed me to work. I promptly got a job as a substitute teacher while my youngest was in kindergarten. A couple of years later, I went back to school to get a teaching degree (his idea). It had the unintended side effect that I started socializing. I discovered I was smart. My classmates would call me for help with homework, and they valued my opinion. As I said – working was his idea, and it was he who pushed me into getting a degree so I could earn more money for our family. But every time I had an exam, he would threaten me with divorce, belittle me, and say phrases like: "You're really going to let your studying come before the wellbeing of this family and our children?" Well, the more of those he came up with, the harder I studied, and along the way my education became my life-raft. It represented financial freedom and social connection. And – most importantly – it represented being valued for who I am as a human being. It saved my life.

We divorced six months before I finished school.

Don't Let Them Break You
By Diesta Kaiser

For all of you out there being abused in any way, don't let them break you, don't let them make you believe that you are less than you are. Get out, run as fast and as far as you can, and if you are afraid of them, ask someone for help. You are strong enough to get away if you only want to.

Never let what one person did to you make you hard with hate, and never blame others for what they did to you; trust me, it's hard, it always will be, but just because one man or woman hurt you, doesn't mean that they all will.

And never stop forgiving yourself for being afraid, or not strong enough at the time to walk away; what matters is that you get the strength to stand up for yourself now.

Survivor Art
Eliska Hahn

Winter
By Faith Ruppert

"What is your problem?!" I scream at the top of my lungs. My grip on the bottle is becoming stronger and stronger and my knuckles are beginning to turn white. Inside of me a battle is taking place, a war between my dangerous temper and my guilty conscience.

I wait in vain for something, anything. A growl from his throat, telling me to stop this nonsense and to put the bottle away. A soft whimper, and a plea not to hit him.

But always, it's this resigned silence of his, this accepted defeat, that infuriates me. Why doesn't he stand up for himself, why doesn't he say something?

"You call yourself a man?" I yell, approaching him menacingly. "Stop crying!" I slap what little is exposed of his face, expecting a yelp.

Silence.

Why can't I push away these feelings of disgust and anger? I am weighed down by guilt, but I cannot stop myself from hurting him.

I hear a sound of mangled emotion escape me, a sound full of misdirected anger and unfulfilled hope. The bottle shatters into a million pieces over his head as I slam it against the wall.

"Just get out of here!" I say curtly, and I notice that hot tears are now running down my own cheeks. I hang my head in shame.

He gets up hesitantly.

"Go on, hurry up and get out!" I yell again, fists clenched in regret.

"Lyn," he says in a sweet tone. He's finally speaking, but not in anger and not in fear. "Please, forgive me. I don't even know that girl's name, you know I-"

"Shut up!" I scream, cutting him off. I am the one sobbing now. I'm the hypocrite.

Why is he being sweet to me? What have I done to deserve it? Why does he stay with me like this?

Why do I direct my anger at him, when the person I hate most in this world is myself? I am a horrible, angry, ugly person.

Now I desperately want to say that I'm sorry, to beg him not to leave me. But my mouth is clamped shut, and he slinks away sadly, with a sigh that nearly breaks my heart.

When he is gone, I collapse on the ground into a thunderstorm of tears. Will I ever be able to escape the shame? Will we ever get out of this mess?

My legs are fidgety as Ms. Bea hands us the poorly photocopied lesson. I sit uncomfortably close to my classmates on this sofa, because some psychologist decided that teenagers learn about sex and drugs more effectively when crowded on a couch than when alone in desks.

I don't even look at the handout. Lifeskills class doesn't count for a grade, so I'm not particularly interested in another diagram of the male anatomy.

"Alright, children," Ms. Bea begins. "Today's topic is going to be domestic violence."

Suddenly the photocopy is crushed as my fist clutches it with urgency, and it makes a loud crumpling sound.

She clears her throat and begins her scripted monologue, which she shamelessly reads off of a department-prepared paper.

"For women between 15 and 24 in the United States," she says, "domestic violence is the number one cause of injury. 25% of American women will experience abuse at some point in their lifetime. More importantly, nearly 75% of Americans know a woman who has suffered abuse in a relationship."

She puts the paper down. I'm starting to feel sick.

"It's important here at Sam Adams High that we create an environment where women are respected and have an opportunity to voice any abuse they might be experiencing," she says.

I wonder how long she practiced this speech.

"Alright, children. We're going to do a quick survey. Everybody, close your eyes and bow your heads. If you know a woman who has suffered domestic abuse, be it a friend, family member, or yourself, go ahead and raise your hand."

She didn't say anything about women who perpetrated violence. Were they supposed to raise their hands, too?

My hand stays down and I wait in agonizing silence for the exercise to be over.

This is the longest half hour of my life.

There are testimonials. Caroline talks tearfully of her parents. It's well known that Caroline comes from a broken family. It's also well known that Caroline is a convincing liar. She is surrounded by sympathetic comforts and tears; I turn my head away in disgust.

Why is it, I wonder. Why is it that Noel stays so silent? Would nobody believe him? Whoever heard of a man being beaten by a woman instead of the other way around?

I bite my lip.

More importantly, I wonder... why me?

He can just walk out on me. People have told him I'm not suited for him, so why does he bother? Does he feel trapped, like Ms. Bea says abuse victims do?

I clench my fists tightly and stare at my lap.

Does he hate me?

I don't want him to hate me!

He's supposed to be trapped, but I am the one who feels cornered. I've never hit him physically, and today was the first time I ever attempted to assault him; but the verbal abuse is relentless. I just get so angry with him, and half the time I'm not even sure why. I call him ugly, faggot, worthless, useless. Words I want to call myself.

He's a guy, right? That's always my justification. He can take it like a man, surely such petty words can't hurt him. But I know that's not true.

I look at the handout and squint my eyes at the tiny lettering.

"Verbal abuse is often overlooked as a harmful factor in an abusive relationship. Verbal battering often leads to psychological problems later on in the victim's life, such as low self-confidence, feelings of insecurity, and a fear of speaking or socializing with others."

Everybody's been talking about it lately. How Noel has been losing his edge. He used to be the team hero, and now he is having difficulty forming sentences. His parents are worried. Nobody knows what's wrong with him.

I feel completely separated from everyone here. Nobody understands anything about this topic, nobody understands what it feels like to be Noel.

Nobody understands what it feels like to be me.

"If one of you ever falls into a abusive relationship, know that we're here to support you," Ms. Bea drones. "It's important to remember that no matter how much you think someone loves you, if they abuse you, you must leave them. If they really loved you, they would never hurt you."

I'm shaking by now, and the friend on my left has noticed.

"Lyn?" she asks quietly, and I try to hide behind my bangs.

Suddenly Ms. Bea is off the script and personal opinion is flying through the air.

"Honestly," she says in a condescending tone, "People like that never change. They're violent, they're angry, and they're insecure. Don't let yourself be victim to that...."

"Lyn?" Now it's two, three concerned voices on all sides.

I'm trapped, trapped on this couch... they're crowding me and I can't get away....

"Lyn, what's the matter?"

"Are you okay?"

"They take their own insecurities and anger out on their victims. It doesn't matter if they keep apologizing, they always relapse into violence. They're often...."

"She's crying!"

"Lyn?!"

I can feel the whole room looking at me, and their eyes are like daggers boring into my soul. But that ignorant woman just keeps droning. And talking. And ranting. What does she know?! What do any of them know about anything?!

"SHUT THE HELL UP!" I scream, standing up and exposing my tear-streaked face to the universe.

Ms. Bea is startled, but quickly narrows her eyes at me.

"Excuse me, what did you just say to your teacher? Would you like to repeat that for-"

"I would! Shut your ignorant damn mouth! Stop reading off of a script somebody else wrote for you, and stop inserting your biased opinions! You don't know what the hell you're talking about, so shut up!"

She looks stunned and doesn't say anything for a moment.

People begin to whisper amongst each other and I can feel the judgment, the condescension. I want to pin Bea against the wall, I want to throw that wench, Caroline, out the window. It's the same anger I feel with Noel, this anger that causes me to lash out with violent words and empty threats.

Someone says timidly, "Are you a victim, Lyn? Do you have no one you can talk about it with?"

I whip my head around, but am unable to locate the inquirer.

Suddenly the room is holding its breath, waiting for my answer.

That's right, isn't it? I am all alone. There are no foundations to help those people who are the perpetrators, are there? The only place we belong is in jail, because we're despicable, heartless monsters with no feelings.

I stare at my shoes.

Even if there was such a foundation.... If I ever went there, I would be the only woman in the room.

"You could say that," I reply softly. I am a victim. A victim of myself. For me, there will be no help or sympathy.

And if there was, can I really say I would accept it?

Leave me, Noel. Leave me and find a better life.

Gripping chain link is always therapeutic for me. I stare out into the vast expanse of white snow that covers the field, as the icy cold seeps through my body. I don' t have a coat on, but I don't really care.

This is where I first saw him.

It was spring then. The field was alive, vibrant with color and bodies in motion. There is a wall adjacent to the fence I am gripping, and the lacrosse players would often bounce the ball against it and use it to practice their catches whilst shouting to each other in excitement.

That's right. Noel is a lacrosse player.

I barely break five feet.

He doesn't have to fear these frail hands of mine, for they have no real power. I remember the look on his face when I swung that broken bottle at him. He could have picked me up and strangled me in self-defense, snuffed out my life in an instant.

Everyone would have labeled me the victim if he'd done that, even if I started it, even if he'd only been defending himself. Just because I'm a woman.

But he just looked at me sadly and shook his head. And that one act of subordination was what made me angriest of all. If he'd slapped me across the face or called me an expletive, I would have cried in his arms and begged for forgiveness.

I ask God absent-mindedly if I will ever be able to escape this place I have put myself in. This hellish cycle of love and hate which never seems to end.

"Lyn?"

I jump at the sound of his voice and pick up my head, startled.

"Noel?"

He appears from behind the concrete wall next to the fence, looking very bundled up and carrying his lacrosse gear.

"Lyn, why are you crying?" he asks. His face is full of concern and his gloved hand reaches out to me from the other side of the chain link. Even after all I've done, he still reaches out to me with that hand, seemingly asking for my acceptance, for reconciliation.

I remember when spring changed to summer and our relationship grew stronger. Our love had been a whirlwind of happiness at first, and it slowly progressed into fiery passion. And then autumn came, and I began to get worried.

I grew angrier with each day. Things weren't so hot between my parents, and I found myself putting a hole in the drywall one morning. Noel began to practice against the gym wall more and more, although lacrosse season was long over. He always threw the ball around to calm himself.

Now it's winter, and we find ourselves laying in the wake of destruction. Our relationship is in tatters, and I know it's my fault. For him to practice out here in the snow means that his nerves are truly shot. Lacrosse has become his last resort, his desperate attempt to make sense of his world.

"Noel?" I ask softly.

"Yes?"

"Do you hate me?"

He grips the chain link tightly with his gloved hand. "How can you say that?" he asks.

I look up at the tall fence between us and wonder if we'll ever be able to cross it. I've put up this wall of anger and distrust, and now I doubt I'll ever be able to make it to the other side. His eyes, which were once so animated and full of life, are now dull and listless. I've made him this way. I've beaten him down to the point where he can't recover anymore.

"Noel?"

"Yes?"

"Won't you hold my hand?" I ask.

He removes his glove and tries to stick it through the link, but his hand is too big. He's probably anticipating the anger in my eyes and looks away, softly mumbling, "I'm sorry...."

This time, I don't yell.

It's too late for him to save himself. Only I can reach through this wall I have created. I can only hope he doesn't walk away from me, because if he runs now, the fence will keep me from chasing him and I'll lose him forever.

My tiny white hand pokes through the fence and I reach out to him with all my heart. He hesitates at first, as if I am going to slap him with it, and I cringe at his fearful gaze. Will he walk away from me? Will he spurn me and reject this gesture, which has taken all my strength to give? Will he abandon me, the abuser, the person everyone says will never change, the person they say he'd be stupid to stay with?

I hope he does. It's what he should do.

I close my eyes and wait with bated breath.

When I feel his hand grasp mine and open my eyes, a small but warm smile has returned to his lips.

I can only hope that he won't let go, that he won't lose hope, until it is spring again. But somehow, I doubt it.

This is No New Tale

By Virginia Jekanyika

This is no new tale
Just another life to tell of
Tear-stained faces,
Bloodshot eyes,
Wailing, singing, drumbeats
Another loud, sad African funeral

Deep, painful wounds secretly kept
Carefully hidden behind polite conversations
Unimaginable heartache, misery and scars
Bottled up in the heart of a loyal wife.
For she was taught that silence calms an angry storm,
Taught to be silent, not to cause shame
So of course today she lies in the morgue –
SILENT

Crying out to God
Crying out for vengeance
The terrible stench of her innocent blood
Filling the nostrils of all the people who heard,
Enraging them, disgusting them
Yet,
Paralyzing them from action

Because of
His psychological and emotional need to control
Because of our eyes
Dimmed by complacency
Friends, not friendly enough to ask,
To talk, to question – SOMETHING!

All that remains are
A thorn in the flesh
That was left to rot,
A deranged mind
That was never corrected,
Traditional teachings in need of revision,
Loved ones
That never got involved,
A cry for help
That was never cried

Look through reasoning eyes
Listen with your heart
Speak out, help out
Make this tale an old tale
Make this woman the last.

Freedom

By Jennifer-Crystal Johnson

Stuck in that place
That oppressing life;
And all I ever wanted
Was to be happy....

I loved you;
In some ways, I still do....
But now,
You've lost your precious
Control over me,
Over the situation.

I still ask myself
Why I went back to you,
And the answer is so simple:

I thought you would change.
I loved you,
And I thought things might be
Better for us....

For a while,
The weather was
Beautiful;
Warm and bright,
Untainted by
Any clouds in the sky.

Then everything
Went back to how it was.
My discontent,
And all your
Negative everything.

I know that I am destined
For something so much more;
And all you ever wanted
Was to keep me in a cage.

So I broke free.

Just Because: A Poem Against All Abuse
By Timothy Pina

Just because...
You've been stabbed through your heart once, doesn't mean you have to go out and destroy another.

Just because...
You've been abused in life, doesn't mean you have to go out and abuse others.

Just because...
Others have turned your world upside down in pure misery, doesn't mean you have to live in that misery forever.

Just because...
You lived in a war-torn environment for so long, doesn't mean you have to be a war monger.

Just because...
A bastard once broke your heart, doesn't mean you also have to be a heartbreaker.

Just because...
Despair and grief have destroyed your entire world, doesn't mean you shouldn't try to comfort others that are going through their worst of times.

Just because...
You have been treated like garbage in your life, doesn't mean you always have to throw it back at others and treat them the same!

We all know that the cemeteries are full with people who have no problems, pain, or strife.

No one ever promised us that this ride we call life would ever be simple or nice.

Yet one thing is for sure in life: greatness is not measured by how long you lived but by how you lived instead.

Tough times never last but tough people do.

Violence will always breed violence and hatred will always breed hatred, too.

The difference between dreamers and great ones is that the great ones can always perceive beyond their dark clouds of despair and struggles to see the rainbow of hope in their lives.

What goes around comes around, that has been written in the stars.

If you try to plant seeds of true love and kindness,
Your blessing will never be too far.

So be great in your life by dreaming way beyond human expectations.
Make sure to keep spreading your love and kindness from nation to nation.
Always, live your life with love and passion, dare to believe in yourself and watch
Your dreams come true.

If it can happen to me in my lifetime, my friends, then it can surely happen to you.

What She is Worth
By Katie Rendon Kahn

He says he values her.
He picks the gold dust from
every chamber of her heart,
leaving no silver lining.
Bankrupts every branch of
her olive-bearing gestures.
He bounces every
check she balances.

He treasures her.
He picks diamonds
from her tears
and rubies from
her busted lips.
He mines sapphires
with the back of his hand.
Emeralds surface in his wake.

He consumes her.
He harvests her every grain,
slurps the last drops
from her reservoir,
gorges himself on the fruits
of her labor,
reaping everything
she sows.

He needs her.
He sucks the air
from her lungs,
plants his seeds
into her womb.
She sustains him,
though neither seem to comprehend,
how much she is worth.

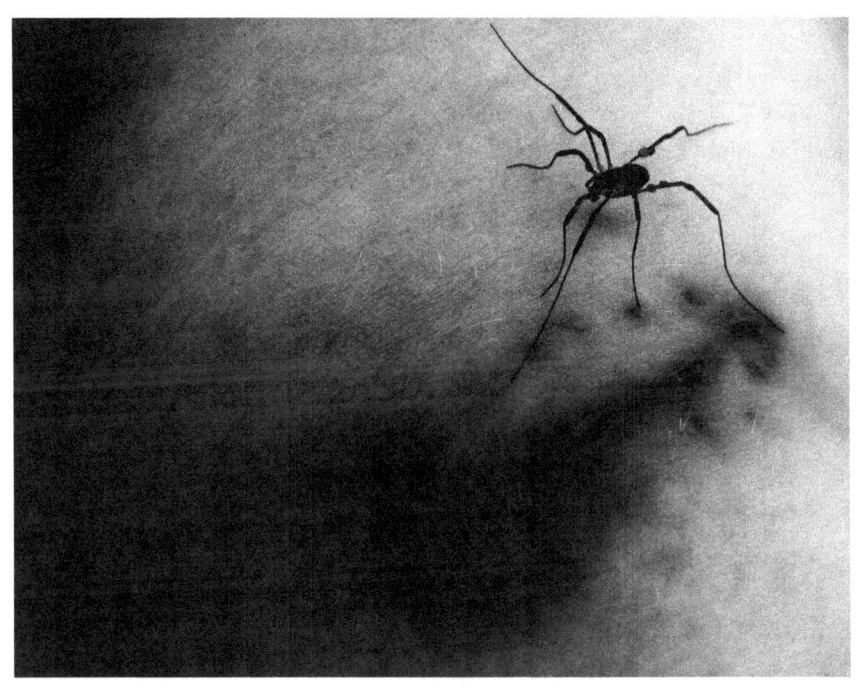

Knit with Silk
Eleanor Leonne Bennett

Tell-Tale Signs & Solutions
By Henriette Eiby Christensen

Five Tell-Tale Signs of a Bad Relationship

1. You are nervous around him. (Walking on eggshells.)
2. His needs come first. (You drop everything at his call.)
3. Your friends and family disappear. (They aren't good enough for you – he says.)
4. You suffer from various stress and anxiety symptoms. (Stomach and headaches, insomnia, dizziness, depression etc.)
5. You complain to yourself or other people about him.

And Five Ways to Start Helping Yourself

1. Take a minute to breathe and do nothing.
2. Do something nice for yourself every day – even if it is just picking a flower, gazing out the window for a few extra minutes or eating an apple really slowly savoring the taste, smell and the beauty. Plan it a day ahead so you have something to look forward to.
3. Call a long lost friend or family member and go out for coffee or a walk.
4. Talk to a therapist or your family doctor – if that is out of the question – Google PTSD and read about it. You can develop PTSD from being bullied – it doesn't have to take a war.

And the toughest one:

5. Listen to yourself. Really listen. Are you willing to live like this for the rest of your life?

Why is this the toughest one? Because you will have to face yourself – honestly – maybe for the first time ever. When I did this I almost became suicidal – if that happens you'll know that you need to change something and you will need help.

Contributor Information:
(in alphabetical order by first name)

Bernard Hafeli

... has published three short stories: *Big Jim* in The Rejected Quarterly, *Guerrilla Marketing* in The Berkeley Fiction Review, and *Down the Road a Piece* in 34th Parallel. A fourth, *Don't Ask*, will shortly appear in Ampersand, and a fifth, *Rest Area*, is under the final stages of consideration at Epiphany. He has also published one poem: *Snow Covers the Dead* in The Hiram Poetry Review. In 2006, he received his MFA in Writing from the University of San Francisco. Since then he's completed two novels, *Grace* and *Scavenging*, a novella, *Bear Season*, and is currently working on a third novel, tentatively called *The Opposite of Oz*, which includes four novellas set in and around Detroit. He also has a short story collection titled *Trail Etiquette*.

Bob McNeil

... is a writer and spoken word artist of some modest renown. His books, *Secular Sacraments* and *The Nubian Gallery*, can be found in numerous bookstores, libraries, and universities. At present, Bob's CD, *Rapping You with the Facts*, is available to the general public. For more information about his literary and recital endeavors, kindly refer to Facebook, YouTube, or mcneil_bob@yahoo.com.

Brenda L. Turner

(No bio information submitted.)

D. Smith

... is the author of a collection of poetry and prose, *Cold Stories*, and lives in Alabama with his wife, Bridget.

Deborah R. Majors

Residing on 30 country acres in the Florida Panhandle, Deborah is a wife and mother of 2 grown sons, and intends to return to college to seek a degree in psychology. Her poems in this anthology are not autobiographical, but as an associate pastor, her insights come through counseling and listening to the stories of others whom she endeavors to help. Deborah has had poems and short stories published or forthcoming in Blackwater Review, Haggard and Halloo

Publications, Barefoot Review, and Time of Singing. She loves writing, family get-togethers, black-and-white movies, and watching the barn-swallows build a nest on her front porch.

Diesta Kaiser

(No bio information submitted.)

E. K. Keith

... has published poetry in phati'tude, Nerve Cowboy, and the Sparring with Beatnik Ghosts Anthology. She loves poetry and organizes events in San Francisco.

Eleanor Leonne Bennett

... is a 16-year-old photographer and artist who has won contests with National Geographic, The Woodland Trust, The World Photography Organisation, Winstons Wish, Papworth Trust, Mencap, Big Issue, Wrexham Science, Fennel and Fern, and Nature's Best Photography. She has had her photographs published in exhibitions and magazines across the world including the Guardian, RSPB Birds, RSPB Bird Life, Dot Dot Dash, Alabama Coast, Alabama Seaport, and NG Kids Magazine (the most popular kids magazine in the world).

She was also the only person from the UK to have her work displayed in the National Geographic and Airbus run See The Bigger Picture global exhibition tour with the United Nations International Year Of Biodiversity, 2010. She is the only visual artist published in the Taj Mahal Review, June 2011, and the youngest artist to be displayed in Charnwood Art's Vision '09 Exhibition and New Mill's Artlounge Dark Colours Exhibition.

For more information, please visit:
http://eleanorleonnebennett.zenfolio.com

Eliska Hahn

Eliska's theory for living life is similar to the average buffet restaurant patron: "You have to try a little bit of everything to get your money's worth." Eliska has had a variety of careers that include radio personality, professional figure skater/coach, activist, artist, butcher, baker, and candlestick maker. She is that eccentric (which we all know is politically correct for "bat-shit crazy") woman in the grocery store comparing apples to oranges, singing Lady Gaga, and trying to figure out how to spell onomatopoeia all at the same time. She dances to the beat of her own drum (literally, she played the drums), and doesn't care who watches. Eliska loves shoes, giving her unsolicited opinion, and her mini-dachshunds. Disclaimer: She tells it like it is. No sugar-coating. Except on her organic banana tartlets, of course.

You can visit her at her blog and follow her most fleeting of thoughts on Twitter.
http://anaudienceofone1.blogspot.com/
https://twitter.com/#!/EliskaHahn

Enigma
(No bio information submitted.)

Faith Ruppert
(No bio information submitted.)

Frances Pauli
Despite a tragic predilection to paint, Frances finally discovered her calling as a writer sometime in her mid thirties. She set aside her degree in visual art, packed up the easel and opened her laptop.

As a lifetime reader of Science Fiction and Fantasy, the stories that clamor for her attention inevitably fall into the Speculative Fiction category. Her tales might feature aliens, fairies, or an oddball assortment of humans, but usually contain at least a trace of humor and often a dash of romance.

She currently resides in Washington State with her husband, two small children, and a host of unusual and exotic pets. When not wrangling toddlers or writing like mad, she can be heard bemoaning her lack of free time to spend rock hounding, belly dancing, painting (yes, still), or enjoying quiet time with her family.

Frances eats far too much chocolate, drinks far too little wine, and does her best to get the stories out and on paper before they drive her completely insane.

For more information or to connect:
http://francespauli.com/

Henriette Eiby Christensen
... was born in 1962 and is Danish. She lived in the USA from 1984 to 1990. Her titles include Author, Speaker, Blogger, Artist,

Teacher, and Counselor. She is a single mother of three and twice divorced, which is why she knows what she is talking about when it comes to what *not* to do relationship-wise.

Violence is not always visible, and although she read Fay Weldon in the 1980's and Robin Norwood in the 1990's, she had to go through decades of misery before getting it. She has a way of simplifying it so everybody can understand – because all it really takes, she says, is for you to listen to your gut feeling – it never lies.

It took her 12 years to get out of marriage number two and five more years to figure out what happened. She hopes to spare you all of that and to be able to make you aware of how you feel, and thus find the strength to not move in, or to move on much sooner than she did because chances are – he/she won't change. Almost anyone can become attracted to someone with a toxic personality. Almost anyone can get stuck in a bad relationship. Why, and how can you avoid it? She answers that in her 110 Ways books.

For more information:
www.110ways.com
https://www.facebook.com/110Ways

henry 7. reneau, jr.

... has been published in various journals/anthologies, among them Subliminal Interiors Literary Arts Magazine; The Chaffey Review; The View From Here; FOLLY Magazine; Entering; Tule Review; BlazeVOX; phati'tude Literary Magazine; Forty Ounce Bachelors; Suisun Valley Review; and Tidal Basin Review. He has also self-published a chapbook entitled *13hirteen Levels of Resistance*. His favorite things are Rottweilers, books relevant to a concealed, but actual, reality, his "fixie," and Ben & Jerry's New York Super Fudge Chunk.

Jennifer-Crystal Johnson

... is originally from Germany, but was raised all over. She has published one novella under her former last name, The Outside Girl: Perception is Reality (Publish America, 2005 - this book is out of print), a poetry book, Napkin Poetry (Broken Publications, 2010), and a collection of poetry, art, and prose called Strangers with Familiar Faces (Broken Publications, 2011). Her poem, Yin & Yang, was featured on Every Writer's Resource's Poem a Day site. One of her short stories, The Clinic, has been featured in Jack Meets Jill, and her short horror story, The Huntress, has been featured in Zombie Coffee Press. One of her short stories, *Shrapnel*, was a finalist in the 2011 Elephant Prize for Short Fiction contest through In The Snake Magazine. Her poetry has appeared in various anthologies including Theatre of the Mind (Noble House, 2003) and Invoking the Muse (Noble House, 2004).

She currently works as the Managing Editor for Phati'tude Literary Magazine published by the IAAS, freelance writer and editor, and is working toward a degree in creative writing. She lives in the Pacific Northwest with her three kids and four cats in a small town near Mount Rainier. Her annual domestic violence anthology can be found at www.soulvomit.com and her publishing company is Broken Publications: www.brokenpublications.com. As of January 1st, 2013, a new literary magazine will be published every 2 months, beginning in February. The site is still under construction, but the magazine will be titled Chronicles [insert story here].

Karen Jones

... is a freelance illustrator in Olathe, KS. http://www.karenbjones.com.

Katherine Shirley

Katherine Shirley is a native Londoner (UK) and near-constant writer of verse, short stories, situation comedy, lyrics, and the odd truly awful joke. Often to be found clutching a notepad and pen perched on the top of a bus, grimacing over speed-bumps and scribbling away, in recent years she has had the pleasure of seeing some of her work brought to life both on stage and in print.

Katherine is fast making a name for herself on the London performance poetry scene, appearing regularly on Tuesday nights at Poetry Unplugged, downstairs at The Poetry Café in Covent Garden. She has also appeared at Farrago, the longest running poetry slam in Europe, and been a featured poet at Howl and Scowl in Hampstead and at the Stockwell Festival. More information about Katherine and further examples of her writing may be found via her MySpace page: www.myspace.com/katherineshirley.

Katie Rendon Kahn

Katie Rendon Kahn is a working mother of three. She spent 10 years married to an abuser and, like a lot of women in her position, convinced herself that it was what was best for her children. She has since reclaimed her life and is enjoying a safer, less stressful life. She is now happily remarried and hopes to help other women find their voices through her poetry.

Kelly Baker

... lives in Los Angeles where she is in her second year of doctoral work in Clinical Psychology with an emphasis on Psychoanalysis and LGBT Affirmative Therapy. She has recently been published in the poetry anthology, *Chorus*, edited by Saul Williams (released September 4, 2012).

Logan Fisher

(No bio information submitted.)

Mari Maxwell

The poem, Recognition, has been previously published at www.dolores-maxwell.com.

Maria Edmonds

... is 34 years old, residing in Hagerstown, Maryland. She is a survivor/witness of domestic violence, childhood (and up) abuse, and a PTSD sufferer. She is a free verse poet and an abstract painter because of the hell she endured. She does not like to give credit where it is not due, however she is accepting that if she would not have burned in those flames, she may not be the person she is today, nor the artist she is today. She considers her writing and art to be self-medication. So many things were taken but not this.

Melissa Salazar

(No bio information submitted.)

Michael Moore

(No bio information submitted.)

Morgan Gallagher

Morgan Gallagher is in her late 40s, and should know better about spending her writing life with vampires. However, she has no choice as they refuse to go away and leave her alone.

Morgan has been writing since she was 12 years old and turned her hand to many things in order to earn her bread. As a mature student, she earned a first class honours degree in Film & English Studies from UEA, studied at Masters level in Film & Television at Warwick University, and has undertaken research into teaching creativity as part of a Masters in Media Education at the British Film Institute. As part of her undergraduate degree, she took several units in creative writing at UEA, gaining 97% for one assignment, a department record. She is also a fully qualified Drama Teacher.

Currently caring full-time for her severely disabled husband and raising her six-year-old son, she spends much of her time in volunteer and charity work, helping support mothers and babies in trouble, particularly those in need of breastfeeding support and advocacy. She has been involved in campaigns to stop child detention at Yarl's Wood Detention Centre and campaigns for babies' human rights. Her lactavist writings are well known and widely circulated and she talks at conferences and events, on both breastfeeding and Film & Television.

Severely dyslexic, none of this is easy. Why does she write? "I don't have a choice. It just is. You may as well ask, why do I breathe?" She is the author of *Changeling*, a collection of short stories called *Fragments*, and a contributor to a number of collaborative works.

For more information, visit:
http://thedreyfusstrilogy.blogspot.com/

Richard Stokes
(No bio information submitted.)

Thelma T. Reyna
Her first collection of poetry, *Breath & Bone*, was published as a chapbook by Finishing Line Press in 2011. They deemed it a semi-finalist in their national poetry chapbook contest. Her short story collection, *The Heavens Weep for Us and Other Stories* (2009), received four national awards.

For more information:
http://www.thelmareyna.com

Timothy Pina
(No bio information submitted.)

Victoria Reynolds

Victoria M. Reynolds is the Spiritual Liberation Catalyst. She is the author of *Transcending Fear: The Journey to Freedom and Fulfillment*, the story of her own transformational journey. Victoria is also working on the creation of several forthcoming books, projects, and films on the subjects of spirituality, co-creation, and core-centered living. See www.victoriamreynolds.com for details.

Virginia Jekanyika

(No bio information submitted.)

Acknowledgements

A big thank you goes out to each and every contributor who took the time to send in their work, fill out release forms, perfect their proofs, and give their words of encouragement for this project. Without the writers and artists who share their stories, the anthology would not exist – I appreciate everyone putting in so much of themselves, even at their own risk, to help raise awareness and reach out to domestic violence victims and survivors.

This is the very first anthology *ever* from Broken Publications, and the first Soul Vomit anthology published. Because it's all so new, I especially want to say thank you to everyone who is taking it seriously enough to respect the anthology, the company, and me. Everything has to begin somewhere, and this is the first step for Soul Vomit.

The goals for the anthology and future hopes and dreams have been made pretty clear already, but none of it will be possible without future contributions from writers and artists, so I hope that these works are received well and that future anthologies will also be received with such immense support!

To learn more about the anthology, Broken Publications, or me, please visit any of the following:
www.SoulVomit.com
www.BrokenPublications.com
www.JenniferCrystalJohnson.com

To follow on Twitter:
@BrokenPublctns
@BrokenPoet

To connect on Facebook:
Facebook.com/SoulVomitAnthology
Facebook.com/BrokenPublications
Facebook.com/BrokenPoetJen

Literary magazine launching in 2013:
www.TheChroniclesOf.com
Facebook.com/ChroniclesInsertStoryHere